GANDHI

GANDHI
THE SCREENPLAY

By John Briley

With a foreword by SIR RICHARD ATTENBOROUGH

Grove Press, Inc./New York

First Evergreen Edition published in 1983
ISBN: 0-394-62471-8
Library of Congress Catalog Card Number: 83-80383

Manufactured in the United States of America

GROVE PRESS, INC., 196 West Houston Street, New York, N. Y. 10014

10 9 8 7 6 5 4 3 2

For my son Paul

Foreword

In the beginning is the word. In the movie business it is true to say that you can never make a good film from a bad script. However one has to confess that it is entirely possible to make a bad film from a good script. If GANDHI should fail it will certainly not be the fault of the writer, since I believe it is based on as fine a screenplay as I have ever read.

Having had my grounding in the theater, my respect for the text is absolute and therefore the filmscript from which I work—always on the supposition that there has been sufficient preparation time before shooting starts—is sacrosanct. Certainly in this particular case I do not believe we altered half a dozen words throughout the entire making of the movie.

Jack Briley has written a screenplay which is both lean and perceptive; it is imbued with humor and emotion, with drama and pain, and maintains at all times a driving storyline, permitting the filmmaker to span more than fifty years in three hours of screen time.

His grasp of his subject is masterly—though garnered in a remarkably short space of time, and his perception of Gandhi has astounded scholars who have studied the subject for much of their lives. Indeed, many have difficulty in deciding whether certain lines emanate from Gandhi himself or from John Briley.

Messages, it is said, are for Western Union. Nevertheless, within the context of pure entertainment, Jack has conveyed the essential truth of all that Mahatma Gandhi said to the human race.

Most scripts do not make good reading but, without doubt, GANDHI is one of the exceptions. Having wanted desperately to make this film for twenty years, my thanks to Jack for making my dream come true are boundless—and so is my admiration.

SIR RICHARD ATTENBOROUGH

A Note on the Text

Darryl Zanuck once said there is no shortage of talented writers, only of talented readers. This is perhaps too generous! But the truth is, reading a screenplay makes demands on the reader almost in the way a radio play makes demands on him—or her. He (or she) must be part actor, part director . . . and only very incidentally a reader.

To a degree this is because the screenplay is part blueprint, part a set of instructions—what is seen in a particular scene, who is present, what is the precise nature of the action. A novelist, focusing on the psychological advancement of his characters, would often skip many of these details, or regard them as distractions. The screenwriter must include them for practical reasons—but at the same time he must present the movie to the mind with a dramatic thrust that enables the actors and the technicians to "see" the film they are going to make. The rhythms, the contrasts—of dramatic action, of night and day scenes, of fervid action and restorative peace, of tension and laughter—all these elements of the final product on the screen are often expressed in "stage directions" and must be "seized upon" in the mind, framing each scene in the emotional and visual context that is often only alluded to in a word or a phrase.

You cannot "lose" yourself in a script, you must "put" yourself into it. But if you do, you can often stage a marvelous movie. You must speak the lines in character—not read them, create the scene, not regard its elements as a list to be scanned.

There are some small differences between the screenplay and what appears on the screen in GANDHI. In almost all cases these are deletions—a line or even a short scene whose import is carried in the look of an actor or the power of a visualized piece of action on the screen.

But these changes are minute. When I first presented the script to him, Sir Richard read every line with a microscope; the two of us examined, discussed and sometimes argued over every single word, but once we were agreed, the movie we staged in our heads was faithfully and (in my mind) beautifully filmed.

J.B.

Author's Preface

Long before I ever became involved in GANDHI, I knew that it was Sir Richard Attenborough's Everest. (To those who do not know him it sounds pretentious to call "Sir Richard" Dickie, but to those who do, it is the only natural way to speak of him—and so, with apologies, I will.)

Several years ago, Dickie was going to direct a script I had written. I think it is safe to say we both loved it, but he could not get artistic control of the project and wisely chose not to do it on any other terms. Even then, in obscure hotel rooms in Rumania, he spoke almost mystically of Gandhi. I listened with amusement. His attachment to the project was so buoyant, so "romantically idealistic"—at least in my eyes—that I was almost grateful I was not involved.

I had a vague notion of Gandhi, a man whose ideas I too admired but felt were wildly unrealistic in a world as harsh as the one I had grown up in. And I was certain that no one in the Detroit of my boyhood or my adopted town in semi-rural England would want to pay to see a film about an old man who sat on a rug in a loincloth and spouted words about peace and passive resistance.

Years passed, and we discussed working together on a number of projects, but always they were deferred by other ventures or news that held out some hope for him that the making of GANDHI might be possible.

And then one day—both of us away from home in a California film studio—he approached me about doing the screenplay for the epic he had labored so long to make. This time he felt he really could raise the money for it.

As flattering and unexpected as the offer was, I had had one or two disasters and really didn't want another—even a grand one. But despite the (by then) almost legendary Attenborough "mania" on the subject, you looked into his eyes and you knew he was far too intelligent, far too knowing to make a film that simply espoused treasured ideas for a world of brotherhood. More than that, he was a man who as actor, director and producer had proven himself the ultimate dramatist. There had to be something there—and from the fun and rapport we had had on that first abortive project I still longed to work with him.

So—with fear and a million practical reservations—I took the plunge into GANDHI. I read the personal accounts, the biographies, as much of the historical record as I could absorb. It was not very promising, but at least I found plenty of incident. My image of the old man on the rug was wrong. Gandhi's long life was filled with action, conflict, personal tragedy and joy. It was, however, even more chaotic and illogical than most of our lives and the thought of reducing it to three hours of coherent drama grew terrifying.

And worse, I still could not understand Dickie's obsession, nor could he quite articulate it. You could feel it! But to one untouched by the magic, it was as hard to comprehend as Gandhi's impact on that vast nation whose millions had come to love him like their real father.

And then, almost in desperation, I turned to Gandhi's own writings. Gandhi was not a writer—not in the sense that Graham Greene or James Joyce are writers. But he wrote almost daily—articles for a newspaper he started in South Africa, and others he later edited in India. And he wrote letters. Hundreds of them.

None of it was "literature," but gradually the personality of this open, questing, unpretentious man began to unfold for me. The well-springs of his courage, his humility, the humor, the compelling power of his sense of the human dilemma—a power which when allied to his striving for decency (and he would put it no higher) made devoted disciples of men as diverse as the cultured, literate Nehru, the cynical Patel . . . and the village peasant who had never been five miles from the mudbrick house where he was born.

And gradually I saw too that Gandhi was not "impractical," not "idealistic." His ideas were forged in painful experience, a growth of perception earned from a life far harsher than anything I have ever known.

At last I understood Dickie's obsession—and came to share it. In writing GANDHI I have tried to make real the brave, determined man I discovered and to show his unsentimental honesty about the complexity of men and his unshakable belief that on balance they are marginally more inclined to good than evil . . . and that on that slight imbalance they can build and achieve and perhaps survive—even in a nuclear age.

Gandhi lived—and I hope the movie of GANDHI reflects—the most fundamental drama of all: the war in our hearts between love and hate. He knew it was a war, a war with many defeats, but he believed in only one victor. That is what Gandhi has given me.

I have tried in the screenplay to give it back in a way that I hope would have won his approval.

JOHN BRILEY

Cast

Credits

PRODUCED AND DIRECTED BY	Richard Attenborough
WRITTEN BY	John Briley
EXECUTIVE PRODUCER	Michael Stanley-Evans
DIRECTORS OF PHOTOGRAPHY	Billy Williams B.S.C. Ronnie Taylor B.S.C.
ORCHESTRAL SCORE & ADDITIONAL MUSIC	George Fenton
MUSIC	Ravi Shankar
CO-PRODUCER	Rani Dubé
IN CHARGE OF PRODUCTION	Terence A. Clegg
FILM EDITOR	John Bloom
PRODUCTION DESIGNER	Stuart Craig
SECOND UNIT DIRECTOR/CAMERAMAN	Govind Nihalani
SOUND RECORDIST	Simon Kaye
ASSOCIATE PRODUCER	Suresh Jindal
FIRST ASSISTANT DIRECTOR	David Tomblin
CAMERA OPERATOR	Chic Anstiss
PRODUCTION MANAGERS	Alexander De Grunwald Shama Habibullah
SUPERVISING ART DIRECTOR	Bob Laing
COSTUME DESIGNERS	John Mollo Bhanu Athaiya
CONTINUITY	June Randall
SPECIAL EFFECTS SUPERVISOR	David Watkins
SOUND EDITOR	Jonathan Bates

EXTERIOR. SKY. DAY.

The camera is moving toward an Indian city. We are high and far away, only the sound of the wind as we grow nearer and nearer, and through the passing clouds these words appear:

> No man's life can be encompassed in one telling. There is no way to give each year its allotted weight, to include each event, each person who helped to shape a lifetime. What can be done is to be faithful in spirit to the record, and to try to find one's way to the heart of the man . . .

And now we are approaching the city, the squalor of the little shanty dwellings around the outskirts, the shadows of large factories . . . And as we move nearer, coursing over the parched terrain, the tiny fields of cultivation, strands of sound are woven through the main titles, borne on the wind, images from the life we are seeking:

British: "Who the hell is he?!", lower-class British: "I don't know, sir." . . . "My name is Gandhi. Mohandas K. Gandhi." . . . A woman's voice, tender, soft: "You are my best friend, my highest guru . . . and my sovereign lord." . . . A man (Gandhi): "I am asking you to fight!" . . . An angry aristocratic English voice: "At home children are writing 'essays' about him!" . . . the sound of massed rifle fire, screams . . .

EXTERIOR. CITY. DAY.

And now we are over the city, coming in toward a particular street in the affluent suburbs of New Delhi . . . there are a few cars (it is 1948), and we are closing on a milling crowd near the entrance to one of the larger homes.

We see saris, Indian tunics, a sprinkling of "Gandhi" caps, several tongas (two-wheeled, horse-drawn taxis) . . . the shreds of sound continue—American woman, flirtatious, intimate: "You're the only man I know who makes his own clothes." Gandhi's laugh . . . The sound of rioting, women's cries and screams of terror . . . An American voice: "This man of peace" . . .

And as the titles end we begin to pick up the sounds of

the street . . . an Australian and his wife, a BBC correspondent . . . all in passing, as the camera finally closes and holds on one young man: Godse.

EXTERIOR. BIRLA HOUSE. DAY.

Godse steps from a tonga as the crowd begins to move toward an entrance-way at the back of a long wall.

HOUSE SERVANT'S VOICE: He will be saying prayers in the garden—just follow the others.

In contrast to those about him, there is tension in Godse's face, an air of danger in his movements.

He glances at two policemen who are talking casually, absorbed in their own gossip—then he looks back at another tonga that pulls up just behind his. Two young men (Apte and Karkare) meet Godse's gaze, and again we get the sense of imminent danger.

They descend and pay their driver absently, their eyes watching the crowd.

Sitting alone in the shadows of a stationary tonga a little distance down the street an elderly man (Prakash) with a short, close-cropped beard and the taut, sunken flesh of a cadaver is watching . . .

Apte and Karkare look back at him. There is just the slightest acknowledgment and then Prakash lifts his eyes to the gate, as though to tell them to be about their business.

THE GATE AT BIRLA HOUSE. EXTERIOR. DAY.

Godse hesitates before approaching the two gardeners who nonchantly flank the entrance. He stiffens himself, cautiously touches something under his khaki jacket, then glances back at the stoic face of Prakash. Prakash's gaze is as firm and unrelenting as a death's head. Godse turns back, wetting his lips nervously, then moves into the middle of a group going through the gate.

GARDEN. BIRLA HOUSE. EXTERIOR. TWILIGHT.

A fairly numerous crowd is gathering here, informally filling the area on one side of a walk that leads to a little pavilion—some devout, some curious, some just eager to be near the great man.

Godse moves forward through them toward the front just as hushed voices begin to remark—"I see him." "Here he comes!" "Which one is Manu?" . . .

Apte and Karkare move to different sides of Godse, staying a little behind, their movements sly and wary, aware of people watching.

Featuring Gandhi. We see him distantly through the crowd. The brown, wiry figure cloaked only in loincloth and shawl, still weak from his last fast and moving without his customary spring and energy as he is supported by his two grand nieces, his "walking sticks," Manu and Abha.

We do not see him clearly until the very last moment—only glimpses of him as he smiles, and exchanges little jokes with some of the crowd and the two young women who support him, occasionally joining his hands together in greeting to someone in particular, then once more proceeding with a hand on the shoulder of each of the girls.

The camera keeps moving closer, and the point of view is always Godse's, but Gandhi is always in profile or half obscured by the heads and shoulders of those in front. We hear the occasional click of a camera, and we intercut with shots of Godse moving tensely up through the crowd, of Apte and Karkare on the periphery of the crowd, watching with sudden fear and apprehension, like men paralysed by the presence of danger.

Featuring Godse. He slides through to the very front rank. His breathing is short and there is perspiration around the sides of his temples. And now, for an instant we see Gandhi close from his point of view. He is only a few steps away, but turned to speak to someone on the other side, and Manu half obscures him.

Godse swallows drily, tension lining his face—then he moves boldly out into Gandhi's path, bumping Manu, knocking a vessel for incense from her hands.

MANU (gently): Brother—Bapu is already late for prayers.

Ignoring her, his nerves even more taut, Godse joins his hands together and bows in greeting to the Mahatma.

And now we see Gandhi in full shot. The cheap glasses,

the nut-brown head, the warm, eager eyes. He smiles and joins his hands together to exchange Godse's greeting.

Godse moves his right hand rapidly from the stance of prayer to his jacket, in an instant—it holds a gun, and he fires point blank at Gandhi—loud, startling—once, twice . . . thrice.

Gandhi's white shawl is stained with blood as he falls.

GANDHI: Oh, God . . . oh, God . . .

Amid the screams and sounds of chaos we dissolve through to

KINGSWAY. NEW DELHI. EXTERIOR. DAY.

Close shot. Soldiers' feet moving in the slow step, half-step, step of the requiem march . . .

Full shot. The huge funeral procession—crowds such as have never been seen on the screen massed along the route. People everywhere, clinging to monuments, lamp standards, trees—and as the camera pulls back from the funeral cortege it reveals more and more . . . and more. All are silent. We only hear a strange, rhythmic shuffling, pierced by an occasional wail of grief. We see the soldiers and sailors lining the route, their hands locked together in one seemingly endless chain. We see the two hundred men of the Army, Navy and Air Force drawing the Army weapon-carrier that bears the body of Gandhi.

And finally we see Gandhi lying on the weapon-carrier, surrounded by flowers, a tiny figure in this ocean of grief and reverence.

THE COMMENTATORS' ROSTRUM. KINGSWAY. NEW DELHI. EXTERIOR. DAY.

Commentators from all over the world are covering the ceremony. We concentrate on one, let us say the most distinguished American broadcaster of the time, Edward R. Murrow, who sits on the makeshift platform, a microphone marked "CBS" before him, describing the procession as technicians and staff move quietly around him.

MURROW (clipped, weighted): . . . The object of this massive tribute died as he had always lived—a private man without wealth, without property, without official title or office . . .

KINGSWAY. NEW DELHI. EXTERIOR. DAY.

As the cortege continues on its way, we get shots of the marching soldiers, of the faces of Sikhs, and Tamils, Anglo-Indians, Moslems from the north, Marathas from the south, blue-eyed Parsees, dark-skinned Keralans . . .

MURROW'S VOICE-OVER: Mahatma Gandhi was not a commander of great armies nor ruler of vast lands, he could boast no scientific achievements, no artistic gift . . . Yet men, governments and dignitaries from all over the world have joined hands today to pay homage to this little brown man in the loincloth who led his country to freedom . . .

We see the throng, following the weapon-carrier bier of Gandhi as it slowly inches its way along the Kingsway.

Mountbatten, tall, handsome, bemedalled, walks at the head of dignitaries from many lands . . . and behind them a broad mass of Indians. For a moment we see their sandalled feet moving along the roadway and realize their quiet, rhythmic shuffling is the only noise this vast assemblage has produced.

MURROW'S VOICE-OVER: Pope Pius, the Archbishop of Canterbury, President Truman, Chiang Kai-shek, The Foreign Minister of Russia, the President of France . . . are among the millions here and abroad who have lamented his passing. In the words of General George C. Marshall, the American Secretary of State, "Mahatma Gandhi had become the spokesman for the conscience of mankind . . ."

In the crowd following the bier we pick out the tall, English figure of Mirabehn, dressed in a sari, her face taut in a grief that seems ready to break like the Ganges in flood. Near her a tall, heavy-set man, Germanic, still powerful of build and mien though his white hair and deep lines suggest a man well into his sixties (Kallenbach). He too marches with a kind of numb air of loss that is too personal for national mourning.

On the edge of the street an American newspaperman

(Walker) watches as the bier passes him. He has been making notes, but his hand stops now and we see the profile of Gandhi from his point of view as the weapon-carrier silently rolls by. It is personal, close. Walker clenches his teeth and there is moisture in his eyes as he looks down. He tries to bring his attention to his pad again, but his heart is not in it and he stares with hollow emptiness at the street and the horde of passing feet following the bier.

MURROW'S VOICE-OVER: . . . a man who made humility and simple truth more powerful than empires." And Albert Einstein added, "Generations to come will scarce believe that such a one as this ever in flesh and blood walked upon this earth."

The camera picks out those who ride on the weapon-carrier with Gandhi's body . . . the stout, blunt, but now shattered Patel, Gandhi's son, Devadas, the strong, almost fierce face of Maulana Azad, now angry at the Gods themselves . . . and finally Pandit Nehru—a face with the strength of a hero, the sensitivity of a poet, and now wounded like the son of a loving father.

MURROW'S VOICE-OVER: . . . but perhaps to this man of peace, to this fighter who fought without malice or falsehood or hate, the tribute he would value most has come from General Douglas MacArthur: "If civilization is to survive," the General said this morning, "all men cannot fail to adopt Gandhi's belief that the use of force to resolve conflict is not only wrong but contains within itself the germ of our own self-destruction." . . .

A news truck is parked in the mass of the crowd. As the cortege nears, the photographers on it stand to snap their pictures. There is a newsreel crew center. The camera features a woman photographer (Margaret Bourke-White) who sits with her legs dangling over the side of the truck, her famous camera held loosely in her hand, unregarded, as she watches the body of Gandhi approach. The intelligent features are betrayed by the emotion in her eyes. For an instant we see Gandhi from her point of view, and read the personal impact it has on her.

MURROW'S VOICE-OVER: Perhaps for the rest of us, the most satisfying comment on this tragedy comes from the impudent

New York *PM* which today wrote, "There is still hope for a world that reacts as reverently as ours has to the death of a man like Gandhi." . . .

The camera is high and we see the cortege from the rear, moving off down the vast esplanade, its narrowing path parting the sea of humanity like a long trail across a weaving plain . . . and as the shuffling sound of sandalled feet fades in the distance we dissolve through to

RAILROAD. SOUTH AFRICA. EXTERIOR. NIGHT.

With the camera high we see a railroad track stretching out across a darkly verdant plain, and suddenly the whistle of a train as its engine and light sweep under the camera, startling us as it sweeps across the moonlit landscape.

Tracking with the train. We begin at the guard's van, dwelling for a moment on the words "South African Railways," then pass on to the dimly lit Third Class coaches in the rear of the train, moving past the crowded Blacks and Indians in the spare wooden accommodation . . . There are two or three such coaches, then a Second Class coach . . . cushioned seats, better lighting, a smattering of Europeans: farmers, clerks, young families. Their clothes indicate the date: the early 1890s.

The conductor is working his way through this coach, checking tickets . . . The track continues to the First Class coach—linen over the seats, well-lit, luxurious compartments. We pass a single European, and then come to rest on the back of a young Indian dressed in rather dandified Victorian attire, and reading as a Black porter stows his luggage.

FIRST CLASS COACH. SOUTH AFRICAN RAILWAYS. INTERIOR. NIGHT.

Featuring the young Indian. It is the young Gandhi—a full head of hair, a somewhat sensuous face, only the eyes help us to identify him as the man we saw at Birla House, the figure on the bier in Delhi. He is lost in his book and there is a slight smile on his face as though what he reads intrigues and surprises him. He grins suddenly at some insight, then looks out of the window, weighing the idea.

As he does the European passes the compartment and stops dead on seeing an Indian face in the First Class section. The porter glances at the European nervously. Gandhi pivots to the porter, holding his place in the book, missing the European, who has moved on down the corridor, altogether. We see the cover of the book: *The Kingdom of God is Within You,* by Leo Tolstoy.

GANDHI: Tell me—do you think about hell?

PORTER *(stares at him blankly)*: "Hell!"

GANDHI *(the eternal, earnest sophomore)*: No—neither do I. But . . . *(he points abruptly to the book)* but this man is a Christian and he has written—

The porter has glanced down the corridor, where from his point of view we can just glimpse the European talking with the conductor.

PORTER: Excuse me, baas, but how long have you been in South Africa?

GANDHI *(puzzled)*: A—a week.

PORTER: Well, I don't know how you got a ticket for—

He looks up suddenly then turns back quickly to his work. Gandhi glances at the door to see what has frightened him so.

The European and the conductor push open the door and stride in.

CONDUCTOR: Here—coolie, just what are you doing in this car?

Gandhi is incredulous that he is being addressed in such a manner.

GANDHI: Why—I—I have a ticket. A First Class ticket.

CONDUCTOR: How did you get hold of it?

GANDHI: I sent for it in the post. I'm an attorney, and I didn't have time to—

He's taken out the ticket but there is a bit of bluster in his attitude and it is cut off by a cold rebuff from the European.

EUROPEAN: There are no colored attorneys in South Africa. Go and sit where you belong.

He gestures to the back of the train. Gandhi is nonplussed and beginning to feel a little less sure of himself. The porter, wanting to avoid trouble, reaches for Gandhi's suitcases.

PORTER: I'll take your luggage back, baas.
GANDHI: No, no—just a moment please.

He reaches into his waistcoat and produces a card which he presents to the conductor.

GANDHI: You see, Mohandas K. Gandhi, Attorney at Law. I am going to Pretoria to conduct a case for an Indian trading firm.
EUROPEAN: Didn't you hear me? There are no colored attorneys in South Africa!

Gandhi is still puzzled by his belligerence, but is beginning to react to it, this time with a touch of irony.

GANDHI: Sir, I was called to the bar in London and enrolled in the High Court of Chancery—I am therefore an attorney, and since I am—in your eyes—colored—I think we can deduce that there is at least one colored attorney in South Africa.

The Porter stares—amazed!

EUROPEAN: Smart bloody kaffir—throw him out!

He turns and walks out of the compartment.

CONDUCTOR: You move your damn sammy carcass back to third class or I'll have you thrown off at the next station.
GANDHI (*anger, a touch of panic*): I always go First Class! I have traveled all over England and I've never . . .

MARITZBURG STATION. EXTERIOR. NIGHT.

Gandhi's luggage is thrown onto the station platform. A blast of steam from the engine.

A policeman and the conductor are pulling Gandhi from the First Class car. Gandhi is clinging to the safety rails by the door, a briefcase clutched firmly in one hand. The European cracks on Gandhi's hands with his fist, breaking Gandhi's grip and the policeman and conductor push him across the platform. It is ugly and demeaning. Disgustedly, the conductor shakes himself and signals for the train to start.

Gandhi rights himself on the platform, picking up his brief-case, his face a mixture of rage, humiliation, impotence. The conductor hurls Gandhi's book at his feet as the train starts to move.

Gandhi picks up the book, looking off at the departing train. A lamp swinging in the wind alternately throws his face into light and darkness.

His point of view. The Black porter stares out of a window at him, then we see the European taking his seat again, righteously. The conductor standing in the door, watching Gandhi even as the train pulls out. Then the Second Class coach, with people standing at the window to stare at Gandhi—then the Third Class coaches, again with Blacks and a few Indians looking at Gandhi with mystification and a touch of fear.

Gandhi stands with a studied air of defiance as the train pulls away—but when it is gone he is suddenly very aware of his isolation and looks around the cold, dark platform with self-conscious embarrassment.

A Black railway worker looks as if he would like to express sympathy, but he cannot find the courage and turns away from Gandhi's gaze, pulling his collar up against the piercing wind.

The policeman who pulled Gandhi from the train talks with the ticket-taker under the gas-lit entrance gate, both of them staring off at Gandhi.

An Indian woman near the entrance sits in a woolen sari, her face half-veiled. A small child sleeps in her arms, and there is a tattered bundle of clothing at her feet. She turns away from Gandhi's gaze as though it brought the plague itself.

MR. BAKER'S LIVING ROOM. INTERIOR. NIGHT.

Featuring Gandhi. As if a reverse angle from the previous shot, he is angry, baffled, defiant.

GANDHI: But you're a rich man—why do you put up with it?

We are in a large Victorian parlor in a well-to-do home. Facing Gandhi are Khan, a tall, impressive Indian. Singh, slighter and older than Khan, but wiry and looking capable of physical as well as intellectual strength, and Khan's twenty-year-old son, Tyeb Mohammed.

KHAN (*a shrug*): I'm rich—but I'm *Indian*. I therefore do not expect to travel First Class.

It is said with a dignity and strength that makes the statement all the more bewildering. Gandhi looks around helplessly. We see Mr. Baker, a wealthy white lawyer, whose home this is, poking at the fire, slightly amused at Gandhi's naïveté.

GANDHI: In England, I was a poor student but I—
KHAN: That was England.

Gandhi is holding a British legal document; he lifts it pointedly.

GANDHI: This part of "England's" Empire!
SINGH: Mr. Gandhi, you look at Mr. Khan and see a successful Muslim trader. The South Africans see him simply as an Indian. And the vast majority of Indians—mostly Hindu like yourself—(*there is a moment of blinking embarrassment from Gandhi at this mention of his own religion*) were brought here to work the mines and harvest the crops—and the Europeans don't want them doing anything else.

Gandhi looks at Mr. Baker almost in disbelief.

GANDHI: But that is very un-Christian.

Mr. Baker smothers a smile.

TYEB MOHAMMED: Mr. Gandhi, in this country Indians are not allowed to walk along a pavement with a "Christian"!

Gandhi looks at Khan incredulously.

GANDHI: You mean you employ Mr. Baker as your attorney, but you can't walk down the street with him?
KHAN: I can. But I risk being kicked into the gutter by someone less "holy" than Mr. Baker.

He smiles, but his eyes show that it is no joke.
Gandhi glances from one to the other of them—absorbing

the inconceivable. And then almost before our eyes his innocence of the world fuses with his anger at the injustice of it all.

GANDHI: Well, then, it must be fought. We are children of God like everyone else.

KHAN *(dryly)*: Allah be praised. And what battalions will you call upon?

GANDHI: I—I will write to the press—here—and in England. *(He turns to Baker firmly)* And I will use the courts.

He lifts the legal documents threateningly.

SINGH: You will make a lot of trouble.

Its tone is chilling, and Gandhi's firmness is shaken a little.

GANDHI: We are members of the Empire. And we come from an ancient civilization. Why should we not walk on the pavements like other men?

The sturdy Khan is studying him with a look of wry interest.

KHAN: I rather like the idea of an Indian barrister in South Africa. I'm sure our community could keep you in work for some time, Mr. Gandhi—even if you caused a good deal of trouble. *(Gandhi reacts uncertainly.) Especially* if you caused a good deal of trouble.

Gandhi glances at Tyeb Mohammed and Baker, then stiffens, plainly frightened by the challenge, but just as plainly determined to take it.

MOSQUE. EXTERIOR. DAY.

We see a rather crudely stitched sign: "Indian Congress Party of South Africa." Gandhi, now sporting a moustache, stands with Khan and Singh near a fire that has been started in the open area before the Mosque. A wire basket has been placed on supports over the fire. Before them, a small crowd, mostly Indian (Hindus, Sikhs, Muslims), but with a few Whites drawn by curiosity. Gandhi whispers, trying to ignore the crowd.

GANDHI: There's the English reporter. I told you he'd come.

We see the English reporter waiting sceptically. Near him, trying to be inconspicuous on the edge of the small crowd, are five policemen (one sergeant and four constables). A horse-drawn paddy wagon is drawn up beside them.

KHAN: You also said your article would draw a thousand people. *(If the crowd numbers 100 they're lucky.)* At least some of the Hindus brought their wives.

We see five or six women in saris standing together.

GANDHI: No. I asked my wife to organize that.

We feature Gandhi's wife, Ba, standing at the front of the women. She possesses a surprising delicacy of feature, with large expressive eyes and a beautiful mouth—but at this moment she is ill at ease and uncertain, forcing herself to do that which she would rather not.

SINGH *(alarmed)*: Some of them are leaving . . .

Gandhi wets his lips nervously. He glances with a little apprehension at the police, then takes his notes from his pocket and moves to the front of the fire. He holds up his hand for attention. He forces a smile—then starts reading—

GANDHI: Ladies and Gentlemen, we have asked you to gather here to help us proclaim our right to be treated as equal citizens of the Empire.

It is flat and dull, like someone reading a speech to themselves, and those in the crowd who had hesitated before wandering off shrug and continue on their way. Gandhi is unnerved by it a little but he struggles on—louder, but just as colorlessly.

GANDHI: We do not seek conflict. We know the strength of the forces arrayed against us, know that because of them we can only use peaceful means—but we are determined that justice will be done!

This last has come more firmly, and he lifts his head to the crowd, as though expecting a reaction. Three or four committed supporters applaud on cue, but his technique is so inexpert that it draws nothing but blank faces from the bulk of them. He glances nervously at Ba, who is embarrassed for them both now. She wraps her sari more closely around her and her expression is a wife's "I told you so"—sufferance, mortification and loyalty, all in one. Gandhi wets his lips again—and takes a square of cardboard from his pocket—his "pass."

GANDHI: The symbol of our status is embodied in this pass—which we must carry at all times, but no European even has to have.

He holds it up. A constable glances at the police sergeant.

GANDHI: And the first step to changing our status is to eliminate this difference between us.

And he turns and drops his pass in the wire basket over the fire. The flames engulf it.

The police sergeant's eyes go wide with disbelief. The crowd murmurs in shock. At last Gandhi has got a reaction, but the dropping of the card has been as matter-of-fact as his speaking, with none of the drama one might expect from so startling a gesture. Even so, a constable glances at the police sergeant again, "Do we take him?". The sergeant just shakes his head, "Wait."

Khan moves up to Gandhi as the tremor of reaction ripples through the crowd.

KHAN (quietly): You write brilliantly, but you have much to learn about handling men.

He takes Gandhi's notes from him, and faces the crowd.

KHAN (the reading not fluent, but firm and pointed): We do not want to ignite . . . the fear or hatred of anyone. But we ask you—Hindu, Muslim and Sikh—to help us light up the sky . . . and the minds of the British authorities—with our defiance of this injustice.

It is the end of the speech. He looks at the crowd. No one knows quite what to do. Gandhi harumphs—gesturing to a shallow box Singh holds. Kahn turns back, extemporizing rather lamely.

KHAN: We will now burn the passes of our committee and its supporters. We ask you to put your passes on the fire with—

POLICE SERGEANT: Oh, no, you bloody well don't!

He has stepped forward with his constables, who have faced the crowd, halting the tentative movements of the few committed supporters toward the fire.

POLICE SERGEANT: Those passes are government property! And I will arrest the first man who tries to burn one!

He is facing the crowd. Behind him, Khan holds himself erect and slowly takes his own card from his pocket. He holds it aloft and then lowers it resolutely into the wire basket. The crowd reacts and the sergeant turns just in time to see it dropped in the flame.

POLICE SERGEANT: Take him away!

He gestures to a constable, who turns from the crowd and marches to Khan, seizing him by the arm and marching him to the paddy wagon. As he passes the sergeant, the sergeant takes his billy club, and faces the crowd, rapping the club menacingly against his hand.

POLICE SERGEANT: Now—are there any more?!

Behind him, Gandhi wavers indecisively a moment, then takes the box from Singh and moves to the fire. Ba holds her hand to her mouth—terrified. Again the crowd's reaction turns the sergeant. Gandhi is at the fire. For a second, his eyes lock with the sergeant's—and then nervously, he takes a card and drops it in the wire basket, and another.

POLICE SERGEANT: You little sammy bastard—I—

He has leapt across the distance betweent them, knocking the box from Gandhi's hands, sending the cards flying and shoving Gandhi to the ground. He turns and faces the crowd angrily, pointing the billy club threateningly.

POLICE SERGEANT: You want that kind of trouble—you can have it!

Again, a murmur from the crowd turns him. Gandhi, on his hands and knees, blood trickling from his abraded cheek, has picked up a card from the ground and he leans forward apprehensively, his eyes fearfully on the sergeant, but he drops it defiantly in the basket. The sergeant's fury bursts— and he slams the billy club down on Gandhi's head. Gandhi sags to the ground. Ba screams. She starts to run to him, but the other women seize her.

BA: Let me go!

She fights loose, but one of the constables takes her firmly.

The sergeant turns from the commotion to see that Gandhi, his head oozing blood, has crawled to his knees again and is picking up another card. The crowd watches. The newspaper reporter watches. Ba stares in anguish. Gandhi lifts the card. The sergeant stares at him, angry but his emotions somewhat in control after the first blow.

SERGEANT: Stop!

An instant of hesitation, then Gandhi drops the card into the basket. The sergeant almost stops, but he strikes again. A quiver of distaste at his own act crosses his face as Gandhi sags.

Ba's anguished face is wet with tears. The newspaper reporter stares without making notes. Khan, at the paddy wagon, watches in wonder.

Gandhi, his head badly bleeding now, rises to his knees—a breath and he gropes around the ground for another card. His fingers finally clutch one.

The sergeant stares, his face racked with uncertainty and confusion.

Gandhi lifts the card and painfully holds it over the fire, then drops it in the basket.

The sergeant slams the billy club down again—firmly, but with a manifest reluctance. The crowd watches breathlessly, the newspaper reporter stares. The sergeant draws a breath, grasping the club, but he bites his lip as he sees Gandhi lift his head feebly, his shaking hands, stained with his own blood, groping for another card. . . .

GANDHI'S BEDROOM. SOUTH AFRICA.
INTERIOR. NIGHT.

Ba is gently removing Gandhi's suit coat, staring fearfully at a bandage on his head, another along the side of his face. The room is gaslit, overfurnished in the Victorian manner.

Middle class. Gandhi sits carefully on the bed, where some newspapers are spread out, English-language ones among them.

GANDHI: You saved the papers.

Ba reaches forth, gently touching the bandages on his head.

BA: I wish you were still struggling for work in Bombay.

Gandhi doesn't take his eyes from the papers, but he shakes his head.

GANDHI: I hated that—all the pettiness, the little corruptions. (A *reflective grin.*) And I was more laughing stock than lawyer.

He smiles whimsically, then turns back to the papers.

GANDHI: But they needed me here. If I'd never been thrown off that train, perhaps no one would ever have needed me.

Ba stares at the back of his head, wounded by that remark, bearing it as stoically as be bore the blows against him.

GANDHI (*reading*): "A high court judge has confirmed that Mr. Gandhi would have been within his rights to prosecute for assault since neither he nor Mr. Khan resisted arrest."—I told you about English law.
BA: As I told you about English policemen.

Before Gandhi can retort there is a knock on the door.

GANDHI: Yes?

A small, round ayah (an Indian nursemaid) pushes open the door and proudly admits her charges, Gandhi's sons: Harilal (ten), Manilal (six) and Ramdas (two). They are all dressed in European suits, ties and stiff collars. They step forward, one by one, making the *pranam* (the Hindu gesture of greeting), then bending and touching hands and lips to Gandhi's feet in the traditional obeisance of child to father.

HARILAL: We are glad to have you back, Bapu.

Gandhi smiles.

GANDHI: And I am glad to be back. *(He holds his hands out to Ramdas.)* Come . . .

And Ramdas runs to him and Gandhi bends to kiss him as Ramdas put his arms around his neck.

BA: Be careful!

Gandhi pats him indulgently, then carefully stands erect, looking at them all with satisfaction.

GANDHI: Tomorrow I will tell you what it feels like to be a jailbird.

The two older boys show the expected apprehension— and interest. Gandhi nods to the ayah. She claps her hands smartly.

AYAH: Come. Come.

The boys bow and leave like boys used to household discipline. The ayah closes the door and we hear their chatter as they go down the hall.

GANDHI: Just like proper English gentlemen. I'm proud of them.
BA: They are *boys.*—And they're *Indian.*

Gandhi is stretching out on the bed, taking up another paper.

GANDHI: Hm. Will you take this off *(he touches the bandage on his cheek)?* It pinches every time I speak.

Ba comes and sits on the bed beside him, maneuvering so that she can get at the bandage.

GANDHI: Here, you see? Even the South African papers apologize—"a monstrous attack."
BA *(of the tape, as she is about to pull it)*: Are you sure?
GANDHI *(impatiently)*: Yes—I can't talk like this.

Ba pauses and looks at him mischievously, as though that's not a bad idea. He scowls at her, then recognizes her "joke" and grins.

GANDHI: Pull!

Ba pulls one of the strands of tape and Gandhi flinches.

GANDHI: Oww!

BA (*mockingly*): Mr. Khan said they called you brave.

Gandhi is nursing the moustache; he looks at her wryly.

GANDHI: If you would let me teach you to read, you could see for yourself.

She leans forward to pull at the remaining piece.

BA: I could have told them you were merely foolish.

Gandhi is watching her as she leans across him, her beauty and proximity obviously stirring him.

GANDHI: It proves what I told you. If I had prosecuted him as everyone advised—even you—they would have hated me—by showing forgiveness I—ouch!

She has pulled the other piece.

BA: There . . .

And she slowly pries the gauze free from the strands of hair above his lip. As she does Gandhi watches her more and more intently, and slips his arms around her back.

GANDHI (*as though continuing the argument*): You see there is such a thing as moral force—and it can be harnessed.

Ba examines the bandage and gently touches the wound, but she is aware of his burning eyes and arms around her back.

BA: Not always. You have told me twice now that you were giving up the pleasures of the flesh.

It slows Gandhi uneasily for a moment and Ba must grin at his discomfiture. He leans back—still holding her, but looking at the ceiling.

GANDHI: I am. I am convinced the holy men are right. When you give up, you gain. The simpler your life the better.

Ba makes a *moue* of acceptance and starts to pull free of him—but his arms still hold her. She smothers a smile and lies down, her face next to his, but neither of them looking at each other. A long beat . . . and then Gandhi turns his head. She is aware of his eyes on her, but she doesn't move. Gandhi leans forward and touches his lips to her neck.

GANDHI: I will fast tomorrow—as a penance.

Ba smiles. Still not looking at him, she places her hand behind his head, gently.

BA: If you enjoy it a great deal you must fast for two days.

Gandhi laughs . . . and buries her in love.

STREET AND COURTYARD OF GOVERNMENT BUILDING. JOHANNESBURG. EXTERIOR. MORNING.

General Smuts—sitting erect and imposing on a beautiful chestnut horse—rides down a tree-lined street. He wears civilian clothes with riding boots and breeches. Behind him, a junior British officer rides as escort. He turns into the entrance-way of an imposing building.

The hooves of Smuts's horse clatter on the cobblestones as the General rides into the courtyard. Two sentries come smartly to attention. A stable boy rushes to take the horse, and a tall civil servant approaches the General busily as he dismounts.

TALL CIVIL SERVANT: The London papers have arrived from the Cape, sir.
SMUTS: Yes—?

The tall civil servant checks his notes.

TALL CIVIL SERVANT: The worst was the *Daily Mail*, sir. They said, "The burning of passes by Mr. Gandhi was the most significant act in colonial affairs since the Declaration of Independence."

Smuts has given the reins to the stable boy.

SMUTS: Did they? Well, they'll find we're a little better prepared this time. Mr. Gandhi will find he's on a long hiding to nothing.

And he strides into the building, past the smartly saluting sentries.

GANDHI'S HOUSE. JOHANNESBURG.
EXTERIOR. MORNING.

Gandhi comes from the house door. He carries a briefcase and is still dressed in European clothes, though far less elegant than we have seen him in before. His mien, the cut of his hair, all suggest a passage of time. As he turns, he stops because he is face to face with Charlie Andrews, a very tall, thin Englishman, who wears a rumpled white suit and a clerical collar. He has descended from a horse-drawn taxi that carries his luggage. He too has stopped. For a moment they both appraise each other, neither speaking. Then

CHARLIE: You'd be Gandhi— *(Gandhi nods.)* . . . I thought you'd be bigger.

GANDHI: I'm sorry.

CHARLIE: I—I mean it's all right. It doesn't matter. *(He suddenly steps forward and thrusts out his hand.)* I'm—my name is Andrews, Charlie Andrews. I've come from India—I've read a great deal about you.

GANDHI: Some of it good, I hope.

He turns and waves to the parlor window. The three boys are there—all bigger—and Ba holds a new addition; they all wave. And Gandhi turns back, and starts down the long, hilly street.

GANDHI *(to Charlie)*: Would you care to walk?

He gestures Charlie on and starts walking.

Charlie nods uncertainly. He looks back at the cab in confusion, then signals the driver to follow and hurries on to match strides with Gandhi's brisk pace.

GANDHI *(noting Charlie's collar)*: You're a clergyman.

CHARLIE: Yes. I've—I've met some very remarkable people in India . . . and—and when I read what you've been doing here, I— I wanted to help. *(He looks at Gandhi, then smiles awkwardly.)* Does that surprise you?

GANDHI: Not anymore. *(And now he smiles.)* At first I was amazed . . . but when you are fighting in a just cause, people seem to pop up—like you—right out of the pavement. Even when it is dangerous or—

JOHANNESBURG SUBURB. EXTERIOR. MORNING.

They have come to a turning, nearer to town, the area poorer, run-down. Ahead of them three youths (twenty, twenty-one) in working clothes, carrying lunch boxes, lean indolently against a building directly in their path. They react to the sight of Gandhi—fun. Then stride the pavement menacingly. One of them tosses aside his cigarette.

FIRST YOUTH: Hey—look what's comin'!
SECOND YOUTH: A white shepherd leading a brown sammy!
CHARLIE: Perhaps I should—

Gandhi restrains him and shakes his head.

GANDHI: Doesn't the New Testament say, "If your enemy strikes you on the right cheek, offer him the left"?

He starts to move forward. Charlie hesitates, then follows nervously, more nervous for Gandhi than himself.

CHARLIE: I think perhaps the phrase was used metaphorically . . . I don't think our Lord meant—

They are getting closer. The youths laughing, whispering.

GANDHI: I'm not so certain. I have thought about it a great deal. I suspect he meant you must show courage—be willing to take a blow—several blows—to show you will not strike back—nor will you be turned aside. . . And when—

One youth has flicked his cigarette—hard. It lands at Gandhi's feet. He pauses, looking at the youth.

GANDHI: . . . and when you do that it calls upon something in human nature—something that makes his hate for you diminish and his respect increase. I think Christ grasped that and I— I have seen it work.

He starts forward again, he is almost on the youths— clearly frightened, but . . .

GANDHI: Good morning.
FIRST YOUTH: Get off the pavement, you bloody—

And he reaches forth to haul Gandhi from the pavement, but—

A WOMAN'S VOICE: Colin! *Colin!* What are you *doing?*

A woman is leaning out of an upstairs window, looking down at the fracas disconcertedly. It is the first youth's mother and her presence reduces the pitch of his hostility considerably.

FIRST YOUTH: Nuthing . . . nuthing. We were just cleaning up the neighborhood a little.

A snickering response from the other youths—but they are embarrassed by the questioning disapproval of Colin's mother's attitude. There's no note of apology in her cold stare at Gandhi, but she clearly believes her son should not be doing what he is doing.

COLIN'S MOTHER: You're already late for work. I thought you'd gone ten minutes ago.

The moment of crisis has passed. Nothing will happen while she is there. Gandhi steps back on the pavement, addressing the first youth.

GANDHI: You'll find there's room for us both.

And he steps around him, Charlie trailing, as the first youth stares at them sullenly.
As they stride on, Charlie glancing back—

CHARLIE *(relieved)*: That was lucky.
GANDHI: I thought you were a man of God.
CHARLIE *(wittily, but making his point)*: I am. But I'm not so egotistical as to think He plans His day around my dilemmas.

Gandhi laughs as they turn the corner.

BUSY STREET. JOHANNESBURG.
EXTERIOR. MORNING.

A busy street in the center of the town. Gandhi and Charlie come around the corner into it.

GANDHI: . . . you could call it a "communal farm," I suppose. But we've all come to the same conclusion—our Gita, the Muslim's Koran or your Bible—it's always the simple things that catch your breath—"Love thy neighbor as thyself"—*(He smiles, thinking back at the youths.)* not always practiced—but it's something we Hindus could learn a lot from.

He has paused before an office and a young girl (Sonja) has come from it to speak to him about something of urgency, but she hovers, not interrupting.

CHARLIE: That's the sort of thing you'll be seeking on this "farm" . . .
GANDHI *(a smile)*: Well, we shall *try*.

And now he turns to Sonja. Behind her we see the small office "M.K. Gandhi/Attorney." Several clients wait, most of them conspicuously poor. Sonja's tone is loaded with foreboding.

SONJA: They're going to change the pass laws.

Gandhi absorbs the news stiffly.

SMUTS'S OFFICE. INTERIOR. DAY.

A strong masculine hand scrawls a signature across a document.

SMUTS'S VOICE-OVER: It's taken time, but it needed to be done fairly. We didn't want to create an injustice simply because Mr. Gandhi was abusing our existing legislation.

Beneath the signature we see the boldly printed identification: *Jan Christian Smuts.*

SECOND VOICE: Just one second, sir, please.

Another angle. A cameraman records the moment with a flash photo. General Smuts, whose presence is equal to his office, addresses someone out of shot as a male secretary removes the document.

SMUTS: But on a short trip, I wouldn't spend too much time on the Indian question, Mr. Walker. It's a tiny factor in South African life.

The reporter who stands opposite him is Walker, much, much younger, almost boyish compared to the way we saw him at the funeral.

WALKER *(a helpless shrug)*: It's news at the moment. I will certainly report on your mines and the economy—but I would like to meet this Mr. Gandhi.

Smuts has risen. He knows how to concede with grace.

SMUTS: Of course. We Westerners have a weakness for these—these spiritually inclined men of India. But as an old lawyer, let me warn you, Mr. Gandhi is as shrewd a man as you will ever meet, however "otherworldly" he may seem. But I'm sure you're enough of a reporter to see that.

The gaze is firm, strong, cynical . . .

TENT. THE FARM. EXTERIOR. DAY.

The sides are half up, but it is dusty and hot. This is where the magazine *Indian Opinion* is printed and we see stacks of it lying around. A short Westerner (Albert West) is running the simple printing press which is powered by a crude generator. A small staff helping him. A Sikh, a Muslim, a couple of Hindus, two young boys.

Gandhi and Walker are approaching the tent from the river, Gandhi discoursing earnestly.

GANDHI: . . . so it's not "spiritualism" or "nationalism"—we're not against anything but the idea that people can't live together.

They've reached the entrance to the tent, and he gestures in.

GANDHI: You see—Hindus, Muslims, Sikhs, Jews—even Christians.

This last remark has been directed toward Charlie Andrews, who sits near them at a cluttered table, typing on an old typewriter. He waves, and Gandhi shouts out to them all over the putt-putt of the generator:

GANDHI: Mr. Walker! Of *The New York Times!*

They nod. One of the Hindus bows with his hands clapsed together. Gandhi hands Walker a copy of *Indian Opinion* and they start across the relatively barren field toward some other tents, Walker glancing at the paper. Gandhi watches him, grinning.

GANDHI: Without a paper—a journal of some kind—you cannot

unite a community. *(A teasing smile.)* You belong to a very important profession.

WALKER: Hm. And what should an "important professional" write about your response to General Smuts's new legislation?

GANDHI: I don't know . . . I'm still searching for a "response."

WALKER *(a leading question)*: You will respect the law.

GANDHI *(a beat)*: There are unjust laws—as there are unjust men.

This carries a weight and apprehension that none of the rest of the conversation has. Walker measures Gandhi with a little surprise.

WALKER: You're a very small minority to take on the Government—and the Empire.

Gandhi seems trapped by an ineluctable fact.

GANDHI: If you are a minority of one, the truth is the truth.

Reluctant as it is, it too carries commitment and Walker senses it. But they have come by a site where a building is being erected, and a European (Kallenbach) is perched above a doorway on the half-completed structure, getting a level. Some Indians are working below him. Gandhi turns to him, light-hearted again.

GANDHI: This is Mr. Kallenbach. He is our chief carpenter—and also our chief benefactor. He has made this experiment possible.

Walker waves his notebook at him and Kallenbach lifts his level in greeting. On his bronzed chest there is a Star of David. Walker looks around, grinning, shaking his head. We see two women in saris trying to quell some squabbling children in the background.

WALKER: Well, it's quite a place, your "ashram"—is that right?

GANDHI: That's right. The word only means "community." But it could stand for "village" . . . or the world.

Walker looks at him appraisingly.

WALKER: You're an ambitious man.

GANDHI *(uncertainly)*: I hope not.

A moment of embarrassed doubt, then he starts toward a half-finished building—wooden sides, door, but canvas still covering the roof. It has an awning spread before it. Walker's carriage is tethered nearby, a Black driver standing in the sun, waiting. In the background we see two women cleaning a latrine. Walker glances at the latrine.

WALKER: They tell me you also take your turn at peeling potatoes and cleaning the "outhouse"—is that part of the experiment?

As we have approached we see a table set for tea under the awning. There are two places. Having set the places, Ba is walking along the side of the building, away from them. She glances at Gandhi tautly and deliberately avoids speaking or acknowledging him.

GANDHI (*a little surprised, a little annoyed*): Ba—we will need another place set for Mr. Walker's driver.

Ba looks at him coldly.

BA: I will tell Sora.

She turns back and walks into the building by the rear entrance. Gandhi is disconcerted by her attitude, but he tries to answer Walker.

GANDHI: It's one way to learn that each man's labor is as important as another's. In fact when you're doing it, "cleaning the outhouse" seems far more important than the law.

A grin—but forced. When a girl (Sora) comes from the building bringing another cup and place setting, Gandhi calls to the driver.

GANDHI: Please come and join us—you'll need something before your journey back. (*He nods to Walker.*) Excuse me a moment.

And he goes into the building, determined to find the source of Ba's aloofness.

GANDHI'S HUT. INTERIOR. DAY.

Ba is sitting sullenly on a carpet near the rear entrance to the building. She does not look up at Gandhi, but she is aware of his presence. He crosses and stands in front of her with all the irritation of a husband. It is hushed, aware that

Walker might overhear them, but bristling with suppressed anger.

GANDHI: What is it?

Now Ba looks at him hostilely.

BA: Sora was sent to tell me I—I must rake and cover the latrine.
GANDHI: Everyone takes his turn.
BA: It is the work of untouchables.
GANDHI: In this place there are no untouchables—and no work is beneath any of us!
BA (*she looks up at him*): I am your wife.
GANDHI: All the more reason.

He holds her gaze as angrily as she holds his.

BA (*finally, scornfully*): As you command.

As she starts to rise he grabs her arm, but she pulls free.

BA: The others may follow you—but you forget, I knew you when you were a boy!

She says it derisively and it stings, but Gandhi is aware of Walker and he fights to hold his temper.

GANDHI: It's not *me*. It's the *principle*. And you will do it with joy or not do it at all!

Ba settles back defiantly.

BA: Not at all then . . .

For a moment Gandhi stares at her, and she back at him, resentfully. He suddenly reaches down and grabs her arm, pulling her roughly to her feet.

GANDHI: All right, go! You don't belong here! Go! Leave the ashram! Get out altogether! We don't want you!

It is hushed but violent as he pulls her toward the rear door, opening it to push her out as she struggles against him.

BA: Stop it! Stop it! What are you doing!?

She lurches free of his grip, glaring at him angrily. For a moment they both stare at each other, shattered by their violence.

BA *(bitterly)*: Have you no shame? I'm your wife . . . *(Like lead)* Where do expect me to go?

Gandhi stares at her breathlessly, his temper subsiding into a dazed remorse. He sinks numbly to a stool, sitting, holding his head in his hands. Ba studies him a moment—and she sighs, her temper and breathing subsiding too. She moves and kneels before him.

GANDHI: What is the matter with me . . . ?

A moment, then she soothes the top of his head—like the mother-wife she is.

BA *(a beat)*: You are human—only human.

Gandhi looks up at her, blankly, abjectly.

BA: And it is even harder for those of us who do not even want to be as good as you do.

And Gandhi grins weakly. Ba catches it and sends it back, warmer, less complicated by doubts. Gandhi sighs, putting his arms around her and she leans into him so that their heads are touching.

GANDHI: I apologize . . .

Ba mutters "Hm" and holds him a little firmer. A moment.

GANDHI: I must go back to that reporter.

Ba nods.

BA: . . . And I must rake and cover the latrine.

Gandhi holds her back so that he can look at her. She looks at him evenly—no smile, but the warmth still in her eyes.

IMPERIAL THEATER. INTERIOR. NIGHT.

The theater is packed. The front rows near the stage are held by rich Muslim merchants, the back of the stalls with small traders, peddlers, artisans—Muslim, Hindu, Parsee, Sikh. The gallery is bulging with indentured laborers—largely Hindu. The mood is restless, belligerent.

On the stage. Gandhi moves forward and he holds up his hand for silence. Seated on the stage are Khan, Singh, three more leaders of the Indian community. Charlie Andrews and Herman Kallenbach sit at the very end of the line of chairs. Gandhi looks around the audience and we see the packed house from his point of view, ending with two plainclothes European policemen conspicuous in seats at the end of the front row. A uniformed policemen stands near them.

GANDHI *(to the house)*: I want to welcome you all!

A buzz, then applause—loud and defiant. When it subsides Gandhi looks down at the plainclothes policemen, fixing his gaze on them.

GANDHI: Every one of you. *(Then, still at them)* We—have—no—secrets.

And again the audience bursts into applause. The policemen just sit like stone—confident, sure, immune to rhetoric.

GANDHI: Let us begin by being clear about General Smuts's new law. All Indians must now be fingerprinted—like criminals. Men and women. *(A rising, angry response; Gandhi just waits.)* No marriage other than a Christian marriage is considered valid. Under this Act our wives and mothers are whores. . . . And every man here a bastard.

In the gallery a rhythmic pounding signals the anger and protest and is taken up around the hall. The police stare imperturbably. Khan leans toward Singh, nodding to Gandhi.

KHAN: He's become quite good at this.

Singh smiles at the understatement. Gandhi holds up his hand, silencing the hall.

GANDHI: And a policeman passing an Indian dwelling—I will not call them homes—may enter and demand the card or any Indian woman whose dwelling it is.
A VOICE: God damn them!

Gandhi just waits.

GANDHI: Understand! He does not have to stand at the door—he may enter.

Now a violent response—a large, powerful merchant rises in the third row.

MERCHANT: I swear to Allah I will kill the man who offers that insult to my home and my wife! (*A guttural cheer; he glares at the police.*) And let them hang me!

Another cheer. When it subsides, Tyeb Mohammed rises near the back, where he is seated with a number of other young men.

TYEB MOHAMMED: I say talk means nothing. Kill a few officials before they disgrace one Indian woman—then they might think twice about such laws!

The police half rise to look back at him, but there is a smattering of applause and several stand to look back.

TYEB MOHAMMED'S FRIEND: In that cause, I would be willing to die!

And now there is general applause. Gandhi waits, then

GANDHI: I praise such courage. I need such courage—because in this cause, I too am prepared to die . . . (*A response; he looks at Tyeb Mohammed*) But, my friend, there is no cause for which I am prepared to kill.

He looks at the audience. This is the more sober Gandhi they have come to know.

GANDHI: I have asked you here tonight because despite all their troops and police, I think there is a way to defeat this law. Whatever they do to us we will attack no one, kill no one . . . But we will *not* (*the climactic point*) give our fingerprints—not *one* of us.

He looks down at the police, making the point stick. There is a tentative reaction from the audience, but uncertain.

GANDHI: They will imprison us, they will fine us. They will seize our possessions. But they cannot take away our self-respect if we do not give it to them.

A VOICE FROM THE GALLERY: Have you been to prison? They'll beat us and torture us! I say—

GANDHI: I am asking you to *fight*—! (*It catches the audience a little, holds them.*) To fight *against* their anger—*not* to provoke it!

He has their attention now.

GANDHI: We will not strike a blow—but we will receive them. And through our pain we will make them see their injustice (*quickly*) and it will hurt, as all fighting hurts! (*Utter silence.*) . . . But we cannot lose. We cannot. (*He looks down at the police.*) Because they may torture my body, may break my bones, even kill me . . . (*Up to the house*) They will then have my dead body—not my obedience.

And now he gets the response he has wanted. Firm, mature, determined. Gandhi holds up his hand.

GANDHI: We are Hindu and Muslim—children of God, each of us. Let us take a solemn oath in His name that—come what may—we will not submit to this law.

He looks at the audience. A second, then a merchant stands, signifying his pledge. And then another. Then Tyeb Mohammed and the youths about him. Then all over the theater they begin to stand and on the stage until everyone is standing. It is all done in silence. Gandhi looks at the full theater—all standing. He takes a step forward.

GANDHI (*a coarse singing*): God save our gracious King . . . Long live our (*the audience takes it up*) . . . noble King. (*And their voices fill the auditorium*) God save the King!!

A prison door slams: we are close on one face, another slam, another face, and again and again in the rhythm of marching feet . . .

MINE AREA. EXTERIOR. DAY.

Gandhi, Singh and Tyeb Mohammed are leading a large procession of Indian mine workers along a dirt road from a mining complex—sheds, elevator platforms, pulleys— toward a distant city.

We see crude, handworked banners: "We are Citizens of the Empire," "Justice for All," "One King—One Law" . . .

Tyeb Mohammed suddenly touches Gandhi's arm and nods ahead.

Their point of view. A canvas-topped open touring car (circa 1910) pulls out from a turning between two factory buildings and comes toward them.

Resume Gandhi. There is a little hesitation in the ranks as the car approaches. In it we can see two uniformed policemen and a civilian.

The car swings across the center of the road and stops right in front of Gandhi.

CIVILIAN: These men are contracted laborers. They belong in the mines.

GANDHI: You have put their comrades in jail. When you free them they will go back to work.

The civilian smiles slowly. He looks from Gandhi to the miners.

CIVILIAN: I've warned you.

GANDHI: We have warned each other.

The civilian looks at him sharply, then smiles derisively, signaling the car off. As it pulls away, Tyeb Mohammed and Singh come up to Gandhi, both made wary by the man's evident satisfaction with what has transpired.

SINGH: I don't think that is very good.

Gandhi watches the disappearing car worriedly, then turns and signals the miners on. They start forward.

Their point of view. The car rides on past the factory building out of which it turned, and suddenly mounted police come swinging out from the buildings and face the procession.

Tracking back before Gandhi, Singh and Tyeb Mohammed as they move forward, fear suddenly making their pace more labored.

Tracking back before the mounted police.

SERGEANT: At the canter—for-*ward*!

They come on fast, batons at the ready. Gandhi screws up

his courage, marching on. Tyeb Mohammed sets his jaw in defiance. Singh forces himself along at Gandhi's side. The mounted police riding on, batons at the ready.

Featuring an Indian miner. He is in the front rank of the procession, watching the horses approach. He has a blunt farmer's face.

MINER (*half to Gandhi*): We should lie down—the horses won't tramp on us. (*Then shouting out*) Down! Down! Everyone lie down!

He starts to go down, and others around him, convinced by the authority of his voice.

The sense of the idea seizes Gandhi, and as the sound of galloping horses nears, he turns and shouts too.

GANDHI: Lie down! Lie down!

And the miners begin to go down, some face up, shielding their faces with their hands, some burying their faces in the earth and covering their heads with their hands.

Close fast traveling, the sergeant's point of view. We arrive at the prone miners.

Close on Gandhi, his arms crossed in front of his face, staring up, frightened, but determined to bear it.

Wide angle. The horses cannot bring themselves to gallop over the human carpet; they rear, plunge, swerve.

Close shot—miner who shouted "down." He is peering through his crossed hands, a tight smile of satisfaction at knowledge confirmed. He turns to see:

The sergeant thrown off his horse. He lands heavily, scrambles up, furious, darts after it. Mounting, he is enraged to hear laughter.

Close shot. Singh and the miner who shouted "Down" kneeling, grinning at the chaos.

MINER: The horses have more mercy than the men.

Singh smiles but suddenly looks up fearfully. The sergeant looms over them.

SERGEANT: You're right!

And without taking his booted foot from the stirrup he swings it into the miner's face. The man goes down, bleeding.

An angry roar from the miners. Several stand and shake their fists. "Bastard!," "God damn you, Englishman!," "Jackal!" The wounded miner himself starts to stagger up.

The sergeant sweeps them, his eyes glittering—*this* he can deal with. But—

GANDHI: Lie down! Lie down!

It is a command, and angry in its own way, but it carries all the weight of his influence on them. They begin to go down again and the sergeant wheels his horse and rides at Gandhi.

With deliberate, almost fatalistic pace, Gandhi goes first to his knees and then sprawls down flat, his hands over the top of his head, awaiting the blow of the horse's hoof.

Close shot, the horse's head, its eyes rolling as it swerves again.

Close shot, the sergeant controlling it, cursing, but unable to make it plunge down on the man.

Full shot, the sergeant wheeling his horse, angrily—surveying the whole of the procession as they lie sprawled on the ground, his mounted police circling in front of them, not knowing what to do.

SERGEANT: Follow me!

He turns his horse angrily and gallops back toward the factories.

Gandhi, Singh and Tyeb Mohammed are looking off at the retreating horses. The car with the civilian has returned in the distance.

Gandhi looks at the miner who first shouted "Down"—a smile, a nod of recognition and thanks. The miner grins, rubbing at the blood on his face, shrugging off Gandhi's implied praise.

Featuring the police. The sergeant wheels by the car with the civilian; his police turn their horses, lining up across the road again.

Their point of view. Gandhi and the miners coming on once more, chanting forcefully. "One King! One Law! One King! One Law!"

SERGEANT: What the hell are we supposed to do now?
CIVILIAN (*watching the procession narrowly*): Let them march.

. . . In our own sweet time, in our own sweet way—we'll get them.

SMALL CHURCH. SOUTH AFRICA. INTERIOR. DAY.

We are close on Charlie Andrews.

CHARLIE: Some of you may be rejoicing that Mr. Gandhi has at last been put into prison.

The congregation is listening to him stiffly, unsympathetically, and there is more than one murmur of assent at his words. The clergyman who has given Charlie the use of his pulpit sits beneath it, embarrassed, but sticking resolutely to his decision to give Charlie a hearing.

CHARLIE: But I would ask you—assembled here in this house of God—to recognize that we are witnessing something new, something so unexpected, so unusual that it is not surprising the Government is at a loss. What Mr. Gandhi has forced us to do is ask questions about ourselves.

A few men in the congregation rise and pointedly escort their families from the church. Charlie struggles on.

CHARLIE: As Christians, those are difficult questions to answer. How do we treat men who defy an unjust law—men who will not fight, but will not comply?

More of the congregation rise and march from the church . . . though a few pointedly do not.

PRISON YARD. EXTERIOR. DAY.

Small, packed. Gandhi is threading his way in a line for soup. But it is a line that winds through masses of prisoners, some with bowls, eating, some not yet in the line.

As Gandhi nears the two stone blocks that hold the large barrels of soup, he sees that Khan is serving from one of them. He too wears a prison uniform and there is a bandage on his head. When he turns and reacts to the sight of Gandhi—

GANDHI: They're sparing no one, I see.
KHAN: No. You were the surprise. It's been all over the prison.

We thought they'd be too afraid of the English press.
GANDHI: So did I.

He takes his soup from Khan.

KHAN *(acidly)*: Don't worry about the meat—it's Hindu *(referring to the soup)*—there's not a trace.

Gandhi smiles, but they turn as the gate opens and a paddy wagon is backed into the press of prisoners. Khan shakes his head.

KHAN: I don't know who they've left out there to do the work. There can't be one mine left open. Have they touched the women?
GANDHI: My wife publicly defied the law. They've arrested her and four others.
KHAN *(angrily)*: The fools! *(He spills some soup.)* Sorry . . .
GANDHI: It's split the Government.
KHAN: Well, that's one victory.

Gandhi looks around the crowded yard at the soiled bandages, the defiant, determined faces.

GANDHI: If we hold firm, it won't be the last.
KHAN: Don't worry—I've never seen men so determined. You've given them a way to fight . . . And I don't think—

He is distracted by a phalanx of guards (an officer and four men) pushing their way through the prisoners.

PRISONER OFFICER: Gandhi! I want Gandhi! Which sammy is it?

The prisoners are moving back from them resentfully but their glances reveal who Gandhi is. The prison officer's eyes fall on him.

CITY STREET. JOHANNESBURG. EXTERIOR. DAY.

A side street, but active. Gandhi—now manacled—is being marched down the pavement before two guards. The prison officer strides in front of them. People in the street stop and turn, staring. That part of Gandhi that is still the dandy is discomfited, but there is a growing part of him that defies appearances.

Featuring a doorway. It is the side door of a large imposing building. The prison officer leads his little procession toward it. He knocks and the door opens The tall civil servant has been waiting for them. The prison officer reaches forward and undoes Gandhi's manacles.

GOVERNMENT BUILDING. INTERIOR. DAY.

The tall civil servant, moving with aloof distaste for his assignment, walks ahead of Gandhi, who in turn is followed by one of the prison guards, toward a grand staircase that is at right angles to them (i.e., facing the front of the building). People working in offices pause to stare at Gandhi as he moves along, more uncomfortably aware of his prison garb than ever.

The grand staircase. The tall civil servant turns and starts up the staircase. Gandhi is even more exposed to everyone's surveillance on the wide, white expanse of the stairway. He hesitates, looking around in discomfort, then follows the tall civil servant on toward the large, white doors at the top of the staircase.

SMUTS'S ANTEROOM. INTERIOR. DAY.

The tall white doors open, the tall civil servant indicates that Gandhi enter. Gandhi passes two male secretaries, and the tall civil servant scoots decorously around him to knock once on the inner doors. Then he pushes them open and gestures Gandhi in.

SMUTS'S OFFICE. INTERIOR. DAY.

We have seen it before when Walker spoke to Smuts, but now we see its full breadth—and the imposing figure Smuts makes as he stands behind the grand desk.

SMUTS: Ah, Mr. Gandhi. I thought we might have a little talk.

He nods to the tall civil servant, who bows and closes the door. Smuts crosses the room toward a small cabinet.

SMUTS: Will you have a glass of sherry?
GANDHI: Thank you. No.

Smuts looks at Gandhi, a little surprised at the frigid tone of that refusal.

SMUTS: Perhaps some tea?
GANDHI (*a shake of the head*): I dined at the prison.
SMUTS: Ahh.

He appraises Gandhi, measuring the irony of his words, his determination. Then with a little sigh at the lost opportunity he replaces the stopper on the sherry, turns and gestures Gandhi on into the room.

SMUTS: Please—please do come and sit down. It's prison I wanted to talk to you about.

He has indicated a chair near his desk, but as Gandhi goes forward he pauses by a spread of papers from England on a long table near the middle of the room. We see one headline in close shot: "Thousands Imprisoned in South Africa/ Mines Closed. Crops Unharvested," a subhead, "Gandhi Leads Non-Violent Campaign." He looks at Smuts. Smuts smiles, a passing nod at the papers.

SMUTS: Mr. Gandhi, I've more or less decided to ask the House to repeal the Act that you have taken such "exception" to.
GANDHI (*a beat*): Well, if you ask, General Smuts, I'm sure it will be done.

Smuts smiles.

SMUTS: Hm. Of course it is not quite that simple.
GANDHI: Somehow I expected not.

A wry smile, and he sits on the edge of the chair Smuts has directed him to. Smuts measures him again, not absolutely certain how to deal with him. A pause, and he affects to take Gandhi's irony at face value.

SMUTS: I'm glad to hear you say that . . . very glad. You see if we repeal the Act under pressure (*a nod at the papers again*) under this kind of pressure it will create a great deal of resentment. Can you understand that?
GANDHI: Very well.

And Gandhi does understand it—as a guiding principle. Never humiliate your enemy. And his tone conveys it.

SMUTS (*a bit surprised*): Good. Good. (*The bland politician: the compromise.*) I have thought of calling for a Royal Commission to "investigate" the new legislation. (*He gestures, implying they'll do what they're told.*) I think I could guarantee they would recommend the Act be repealed.

GANDHI (*waiting for the catch*): I congratulate them.

Smuts does a slight double take, a smile, then the "tough" politician.

SMUTS: But they might also recommend that future Indian immigration be severely restricted—even stopped.

He measures Gandhi challengingly, obviously expecting some contest. Gandhi mulls it, then

GANDHI: Immigration was not an issue on which we fought. It would be wrong of us to make it one now that we—we are in a position of advantage.

Smuts stares at him . . . a moment, then

SMUTS: You're an extraordinary man.

GANDHI (*his grin; he brushes at his prison garb*): I assure you I feel a very ordinary man at this moment.

And now Smuts smiles with him. He bends suddenly and signs a group of documents.

SMUTS: I'm ordering the release of all prisoners within the next twenty-four hours. You yourself are free from this moment.

Gandhi stands, a little uncertain about the sudden change in his status. Smuts signs the last document, then sees Gandhi's doubt—and misreads it.

SMUTS: Assuming we are in agreement?

GANDHI: Yes—yes. It's just that . . . in these clothes I'd—I'd prefer to go by taxi.

SMUTS (*confused by his hesitation*): All right. Fine.

GANDHI: I'm—I'm afraid I have no money.

SMUTS: Oh! (*He quickly feels in his waistcoat pockets—and realizes he has no money!*) Neither have I. (*He reaches forth and touches a buzzer.*) I'm awfully sorry.

The tall civil servant (Daniels) enters.

SMUTS: Daniels, would you lend Mr. Gandhi a shilling for a taxi?

Daniels stares.

DANIELS: I beg your pardon, sir?

SMUTS *(a second thought)*: How far will you be going, Mr. Gandhi?

GANDHI *(a mischievous smile)*: Well—now that this is settled—I had thought seriously of going back to India *(he faces the startled Daniel)* but a shilling will do splendidly for the moment.

Still a little confused, Daniels reaches in his pocket and produces a shilling. He hands it to Gandhi.

GANDHI: Thank you. *(To Smuts)* Thank you both for a very enlightening experience.

He bows slightly and starts out the door. Daniels immediately starts to accompany him, but Gandhi stops. A beat.

GANDHI *(ice)*: I'm obliged, Mr. Daniels, but I will find my *own* way out.

And his own steel shows in the oblique reference to the ignominy of his way in. Daniels bows, and he and Smuts just stare as the uniformed "prisoner" goes out through the grand doors, past the stunned men in the office to the outer doors and on to the grand staircase. The prison guard appears in the doorway, looking off in confusion at Gandhi, then back at the office for guidance. Daniels simply shakes his head "Let him be."

Finally, when Gandhi has disappeared down the stairs, Daniels turns to Smuts.

SMUTS *(a shake of the head)*: He's either a great man or a colossal fraud . . . Either way, I shall be glad to see the last of him.

THE PIER AT BOMBAY. EXTERIOR. DAY.

Ship's siren, military band . . . a jubilant crowd on the pier, passengers waving to the receiving crowd. A group of First Class passengers, ninety percent English, look down from the upper deck.

From their point of view. We see the main section of the

pier, a crowd of mostly European civilians on one side. A mass of military on the other: European officers, topees and swagger sticks, Indian cavalry, Gurkha infantry, Sikh lancers—turbans, rifles, bugles, an Indian military band—a showy awe-inspiring display.

Featuring two Englishmen. First Class passengers, white suits, Oxbridge accents; one quite young, the other a bit older, both civil servants coming to "administer" India.

YOUNG ENGLISHMAN: By God, he loves it. . . .

Their point of view. A British general is coming down the gangplank accompanied by his ADC. The officer commanding and the Guard of Honor await him.

SECOND ENGLISHMAN: I'm sure he hates it.

The young Englishman glances at him quizzically. The General has taken the salute and moves to inspect the troops to the accompaniment of the military band.

SECOND ENGLISHMAN: Generals' reputations are being made in France today, fighting on the Western Front. Not as Military Governors in India.

He is suddenly aware of a well-dressed Indian half-listening to their conversation. He glances at him and the well-dressed Indian simply nods slightly and moves off a little. The second Englishman grimaces at the young Englishman and looks down again.

SECOND ENGLISHMAN: What the devil's going on back there?

He is looking aft. His point of view.
Another far less elaborate gangplank extends from the aft section of the ship. Third Class passengers are disembarking here, and on shore, separated by a wire fence from the rest of the pier. A large crowd of Indians is reacting excitedly to someone coming down the gangplank but we can't yet see that person.

The young Englishman glances back at the well-dressed Indian to make sure of his distance, then speaks quietly.

YOUNG ENGLISHMAN: It must be that Indian that made all that fuss back in Africa. My cabin boy told me he was on board.

SECOND ENGLISHMAN: Why haven't we seen him? *(Finding the name)* Gandhi?

YOUNG ENGLISHMAN: Yes. That's it. He was traveling Third Class. There he is.

Their point of view.

There has been a little hiatus in those disembarking but now Gandhi has appeared, coming down the gangplank with Ba and the children (grown-up sons now), and three or four people behind them, including the tall figure of Charlie Andrews. But Gandhi is wearing an Indian tunic and sandals and he has shaved his hair except for a central section on the top.

SECOND ENGLISHMAN'S VOICE-OVER: God—he's dressed like a coolie! I thought he was a lawyer.

The young Englishman glances back cautiously toward the well-dressed Indian again, then

YOUNG ENGLISHMAN: After he came out of jail he refused to wear European clothes.

THE PIER. THIRD CLASS AREA. EXTERIOR. DAY.

Gandhi is smiling, trying to move on, but answering the questions of an Indian journalist.

GANDHI: No, no, I haven't "refused" . . . I—I simply wanted to dress the way my comrades in prison dressed.

He speaks with an uncertainty and tentativeness that he had lost in South Africa, patently overwhelmed by the reception. An English journalist catches him as he turns.

ENGLISH JOURNALIST: Will you support the war effort, Mr. Gandhi?

An exuberant woman puts a garland over his shoulders.

GANDHI: I—I have demanded rights as a British citizen, it is therefore my duty to help in the defense of the British Empire.

He smiles uncertainly again. As he turns he is face to face with an American reporter.

AMERICAN REPORTER: What are you going to do now that you're back in India?

GANDHI: I don't know. . . . I don't know. . . .

An Indian reporter has cornered Ba behind him.

SECOND INDIAN REPORTER: As an Indian woman how could you accept the indignity of prison?

Gandhi half-twists to hear Ba's answer, but his arm is taken by a young Indian (Nehru) in elegant European clothes. Another garland is thrown over his shoulders.

NEHRU: Please, Mr. Gandhi.

Featuring Ba. Offhand, her eyes on Gandhi ahead.

BA: My dignity comes from following my husband.

She joins her hands, acknowledging a garland placed around her shoulders, and pushes on after Gandhi. Charlie helps to guide her.

Featuring Gandhi. The young Nehru, somewhat amused by all the excitement, leads Gandhi through the crowd to a little flower-covered platform. We see a banner: THE CONGRESS PARTY WELCOMES GANDHI.

NEHRU (he too speaks with an Oxbridge accent): Just a few words—then we'll get you to civilization.

He grins. He has guided Gandhi to the first step of the platform. Another garland is wrapped around Gandhi's shoulders, and in some embarrassment, he mounts the platform. There is a great cheer, but in the silence that follows we hear the military band from across the way as the troops prepare to march off. Gandhi looks around at the crowd. Finally he speaks out.

GANDHI: I—I am glad to be home. (A little round of applause.) I—I thank you for your greeting.

He makes the pranam and starts for the steps. The crowd is a little disappointed, but they manage a cheer and applause.

Nehru is standing next to a heavy-set, well-dressed man (Patel). They exchange a wry glance, "Not exactly a world-beater."

A car door slams. The camera pulls back. Nehru has slammed the door of a gleaming Rolls Royce touring car, the top down. He has seated Gandhi in it beside Patel, taking Gandhi's knapsack. An Indian chauffeur rides in front. The crowd still surges around and Gandhi is looking apprehensively back for Ba.

NEHRU: We'll follow with your wife—don't worry, everything's arranged.

He grins boyishly, in part to comfort, in part unable to contain his amusement at Gandhi and his evident confusion.

PATEL'S CAR. STREETS OF BOMBAY.
EXTERIOR. DAY.

With Gandhi still looking back anxiously, the car pulls off. He finally turns to Patel.

GANDHI: Who is that young man?
PATEL: That's young Nehru. He's got his father's intellect, his mother's looks and the devil's charm. If they don't ruin him at Cambridge—Wave! Wave!—he may amount to something.

There are crowds along the street, and Gandhi—in surprise that they are for him—waves tentatively. Patel waves too but he eyes Gandhi rather critically.

PATEL: I must say when I first saw you as a bumbling lawyer here in Bombay I never thought I'd be greeting you as a national hero.
GANDHI: I'm hardly that, Mr. Patel.
PATEL: Oh, yes, you are. It's been two hundred years since an Indian has cocked a snook at the British Empire and got away with it. And stop calling me Mr. Patel, you're not a junior clerk anymore.
GANDHI (*a beat; still hesitant*): No.

They have come to a main thoroughfare. A crowd still lines the street but it is thin and around and between we see groups of desperate poor, parked on the pavement, staring with blank curiosity at the passing car, but too listless and too out of touch to move from their little squatters' patches.

Patel looks at Gandhi's clothes rather disapprovingly.

PATEL: The new Military Governor of the North West Province was on that ship. Too bad you came back Third Class—he might have been impressed by a successful barrister who had outmaneuvered General Smuts.

Gandhi is staring at the street. From his point of view we hold on a gaunt young, aged woman holding a baby wrapped in rags as threadbare as her sari. Another hollow-faced child leans against her.

GANDHI (*leadenly*): Yes . . . I'm sure. . . .

PATEL'S GARDEN. EXTERIOR. DAY.

A splendid peacock, its tail fanned in brilliant display, lords it on a velvet lawn. A woman in a sumptuous silk sari is trying to feed it crumbs. Behind her, Gandhi's reception is in full spate—silver trays, tables covered in fine linen, Indian servants, a swimming pool, a small fountain, the grounds filled with Indian millionaires and dignitaries gathered with their wives to meet the new hero from South Africa.

A beautiful and beautifully dressed woman (Mrs. Nehru) stands next to her distinguished husband (Motilal Nehru).

MRS. NEHRU (*wittily*): No, I leave practical matters to my husband and revolution to my son. . . .

She nods lightly toward Nehru.

Featuring Nehru who is introducing Gandhi to two men, one tall, slender, ascetic looking, but dressed impeccably (Jinnah). The other with a haunting face—beard, flowing dark hair, the air of a poet or a ruthlessly dedicated radical (Prakash—whom we recognize from the opening sequence in Delhi at Gandhi's assassination).

NEHRU: Mr. Jinnah, our joint host, member of Congress, and the leader of the Muslim League and Mr. Prakash, who I fear is awaiting trial for sedition and inducement to murder.

Gandhi has bowed to Jinnah, now he looks a little startled at Prakash. Prakash grins and makes the *pranam* to Gandhi.

PRAKASH: I have not actually puled a trigger, Mr. Gandhi, I have simply written that if an Englishman kills an Indian for disobeying his law, then it is an Indian's duty to kill an Englishman for enforcing his law in a land that is not his.

Gandhi nods . . .

GANDHI: It is a clever argument; I am not sure it will produce the end you desire.

He meets Prakash's gaze firmly, the first moment we have seen any sign of the Gandhi of South Africa.

JINNAH (*testingly*): We hope you intend to join us in the struggle for Home Rule, Mr. Gandhi.
GANDHI (*a pause*): I—

Charlie Andrews touches Gandhi's arm, excusing himself to the others.

CHARLIE: May I? Mohan—I would like you to meet someone.

Gandhi bows to the others and is led off to an Indian bishop in full clerical robes. Behind him we see Patel regaling a small group with some story of court or society.
As Gandhi leaves, Jinnah, Nehru and Prakash watch him clinically. Except for the servants, Gandhi is the ony Indian male not in European clothes.

NEHRU: He told the press he would support the British in the war.
PRAKASH (*acidly*): That's nonviolence for you.
JINNAH: Is he a fool?

Nehru grins slowly, thoughtfully.

NEHRU: I'm not certain. . . But I wouldn't be surprised.

We get a shot of Ba in a gathering of Indian women. She stands listening, seemingly tongue-tied in the sophisticated patter. And we cut to Charlie introducing Gandhi to a man in obvious ill health, but well dressed, looking like the professor, philosopher and elder statesman he is (Gokhale).

CHARLIE: I lied to you, Mohan, when I told you I decided to come to South Africa to meet you. Professor Gokhale sent me.

Gokhale is pleased, Gandhi amused. He bows very respectfully.

GOKHALE: We're trying to make a nation, Gandhi—and the British keep trying to break us up into religions and principalities and "provinces." What you were writing in South Africa—that's what we need here.

He has offered his hand during this, and Gandhi has helped him from the garden chair he has been seated on, handing him the cane that is resting against it.

GANDHI *(a smile)*: I have much to learn about India. And I have to begin my practice again—one needs money to run a journal.

Another grin. Gokhale has started to walk with him, looking at him intently, penetratingly.

GOKHALE: Nonsense. *(He turns to Charlie)* Go on, Charlie. This is Indian talk—we want none of you imperialists.

It is brusque but affectionate; we know he regards Charlie as Gandhi does. . . and Charlie does too.

CHARLIE *(a mock threat)*: All right—I'll go and write my report to the Viceroy.

GOKHALE: Go and find a pretty Hindu woman and convert her to Christianity—that's as much mischief as you're allowed.

He still hasn't smiled, but Gandhi and Charlie have.

ANOTHER PART OF THE GARDEN.

This is private—beautiful and still. Gandhi walks along slowly, taking the pace of the ailing Gokhale.

GOKHALE: Forget your practice. India has many men with too much wealth—it is their privilege to nourish the efforts of the few who can raise India from servitude and apathy. I will see to it—you begin your journal.

GANDHI: I have little to say. India is an "alien" country to me.

He grins self-deprecatingly but Gokhale persists.

GOKHALE: Well, change that. Go and find India. Not what you see here, but the real India. You'll see what needs to be said. What we need to hear.

He pauses and looks at Gandhi—and for the first time he smiles. When he speaks his voice is thick with feeling.

GOKHALE: When I saw you in that tunic I knew . . . I knew I could die in peace. (A dying man's command) Make India proud of herself.

His eyes are watery with emotion, but he stares at Gandhi rigidly. Cut to

TRAIN. EXTERIOR. NIGHT.

Indian. Steam. A breed of its own.

THIRD CLASS COACH. INTERIOR. NIGHT.

Gandhi sits by a window in the dimly lit coach. Ba sleeps on the seat next to him, another member of the party next to her. Gandhi's solemn eyes are studying the huddled humanity in the rocking coach. People are sleeping everywhere, some half-erect on the benches, many on the floor among the bundles and trunks and bedrolls and baskets. Some have children, some are very old. One old man, sleepless like Gandhi, stares back at him across the shadowed squalor of the coach; somewhere unseen a crying baby is soothed by his mother.

Gandhi looks at the bench across from him. Charlie Andrews, his tall frame cramped in a tiny space between the window looks at Gandhi dozily, a little smile of sufferance, then he closes his eyes again, leaning his head against the rocking window frame.

NARROW STREET. A SMALL TOWN. EXTERIOR. DAY.

Gandhi is carried along in a ceremonial chair borne on the shoulders of some trotting men. The chair is swathed in flowers, and flowers are being showered on Gandhi by the running children and the crowd lining the narrow street. Ba and Charlie and two others are following in a flower-bedecked ox-cart, lost in the mass of people that are swirling around Gandhi.

On a building top a British officer watches emotionlessly as Gandhi and the crowd pass below him. On this building and others we see some of his Indian soldiers watching with their rifles beside them.

INDIAN VILLAGES. EXTERIOR. DAY.

As from a train . . . but the shots are varied: some close of
farmers and water buffalo, and ragged children and women
in colorful saris carrying pots on their heads, and some distant of villages as units, one and another and another.

Intercut always with

TRAIN. INTERIOR. DAY.

Gandhi's face in the window, he and Ba standing, looking
out together, neither speaking. Gandhi writing in the
cramped chaos of the Third Class coaches. Gandhi sweeping
part of the carriage, making disgruntled passengers move as
he tries to bring some cleanliness to their surroundings.

RIVER VISTA. EXTERIOR. DAY.

A broad alluvial plain, the river threading through it, pur-
ple and gold in the rising sun. The camera races with the
train along the river's edge, the reflected sun glimmering on
the windows.

RIVER BANK. EXTERIOR. DAY.

The sun is high and the train is stopped by the river.
People have come out of the coaches to cool their heads
with the touch of water, to stretch their legs.

We see an English clergyman from the Second Class
coaches, dipping a toe cautiously into the water, children of
some British enlisted soldiers wading, splashing, faces alight
with fun.

And, farther along, the parasols of one or two of the English First Class passengers, a woman dousing her neck delicately with perfume. A British officer, tunic unbuttoned,
smoking a long cigar as he walks along in a few inches of
water, his trousers rolled up, his shoes off.

Across the river down from the Third Class coaches a
small group of Indian women is squatted by the river's edge,
washing clothes. Some carry infants on their backs. Some
small children stand near them. Their ritual of washing goes
on, but they are all watching the passengers of the train.

Gandhi stands with Ba and Charlie among the Third Class passengers. Ba cools her face with water. Charlie, his trousers rolled up, plays a tentative splashing game with a skinny little Indian boy. Gandhi is holding a large white head cloth which he is soaking in the water, but his eyes have been arrested by the sight of the women across the river.

And now we see the women closely from his point of view, the camera panning slowly along them. Their bodies are skin and bone. The clothes they wear, which looked normal from the distance, are rags—literally, shredded rags, one hung on another. The children are hollow-eyed and gaunt, staring listlessly at the train. One boy, with a stump for an arm, aimlessly pushes at the flies that buzz around him.

Gandhi stands erect, lost now in the revelation of their poverty. His eyes hold on one woman at the river bank. Though her frail face is almost skeletal, it is beautiful but scarred by a severe rash down her cheek and neck. The cloth she is washing is a shredded piece of muslin. Her eyes have met Gandhi's as he watches her.

Gandhi stares for a moment, a long beat. Then he slowly moves his arm out into the water and, without taking his eyes from her, releases the head cloth he has been rinsing. It floats along on the water down toward the woman.

She looks from Gandhi to it with sudden excitement, a sense of incredulity. As the cloth nears her, she rises and moves almost greedily out into the water to take it. Her hands snatch at it quickly. Then she stands, looking at Gandhi. The infant on her back shifts, its huge hollow eyes reacting to the movement.

Gandhi smiles slowly, tilting his head just slightly to her. And now that she has possession of the cloth, her manner calms again. And she looks back at him, and her lips almost part with a tiny smile of thanks.

Hold on Gandhi, staring at her, fighting the pain in his eyes. . . .

TRAIN. EXTERIOR. NIGHT.

Threading like a lighted necklace across the darkness of a vast plain.

TRAIN IN HILLS. EXTERIOR. DAY.

Climbing green hills—a totally different terrain—and again we intercut, this time the train climbing: a boy and buffalo running a huge, crude grinding wheel, train climbing; farmers in terraced fields, train climbing faster and faster . . . until suddenly with a hoot of the whistle and the screech of brakes it stops!

TRAIN. EXTERIOR. DAY.

Gandhi is leaning out of a window in a Third Class coach. Ahead of him other passengers are looking too; some have jumped down.

Gandhi and Charlie jump down too. As they come clear they can see that a military train of an engine and two cars has been derailed ahead of them. A small troop of cavalry are coming slowly along the line of Gandhi's train toward them.

Featuring the cavalry. They are British and their troop leader is viciously angry.

TROOP LEADER: Clear the way! Get out of the way!

He is swinging his sword, not lethally, but threateningly at the Indian passengers from the trian. His British NCOs are equally angry and deliberately ride close to the passengers, forcing them back against the train.

Gandhi and Charlie step back. And as the troop goes past we see from their point of view a group of Indian bearers, trotting in the middle of the horsemen, carrying two litters—covered, each hanging by straps from a long pole—and each bearing a badly wounded British soldier; one appears to be dead.

OUTSKIRTS OF VILLAGE. EXTERIOR. DAY.

The shadow of a train moves slowly along the ground, a sense of tension and foreboding. We hear the engine chugging slowly. The camera lifts. Gandhi and Charlie stand at a window, staring out grimly. Other passengers are looking off too. Ba is seated, staring straight ahead, her face taut, deliberately not seeing what the others are seeing.

GALLOWS. EXTERIOR. DAY.

Their point of view: On a little hill across from the rail-road track part of a prison wall is visible. In front of it a thick pole is straddled across two others. From this crude gallows two Indian men hang by the neck. One is in turban and dhoti, the other in a tunic. The sound of the train stopping.

VILLAGE. EXTERIOR. DAY.

Close shot. Incense rising in shot. The camera pulls back and back. The incense is burning in a bowl sitting before Gandhi on a make-shift platform set in the little valley be-tween the train line and the little hill where the Indian men have been hanged. A small crowd sits in a crescent before him, Ba and Charlie are bent in prayer on the platform behind him. When the camera comes to rest, the edge of the gallows and a portion of one of the hanged men is in the frame. We know we are looking from someone's point of view near the prison wall.

Finally Gandhi lifts his head.

GANDHI (*at first distant, as from the hill*): I ask you to pray for those who died. (*Closer*) For the English soliders . . . (*a murmur*) who were doing what they thought was *right*. (*Closer*) And for the brave terrorists whose patriotism led them to do what was *wrong*.

The murmur of resistance from the crowd is louder at this. Gandhi shakes his head at the dissent.

GANDHI: It is not my law, it is the law of creation. We reap what we sow. Out there in the fields—and in our hearts. Violence sows hatred, and the will to revenge. In them. And in us.

He looks up.

HILLSIDE. HIS POINT OF VIEW.

The troop leader, on horseback, is on the hill beside the gallows. The first view of Gandhi on the platform was his. Some of his troops are lined up beside him. He stares down at Gandhi coldly.

PATEL'S SWIMMING POOL. EXTERIOR. DAY.

Patel lounges in the water on his back, supported by a large air pillow. Nehru sits at the side of the pool in a swimming suit, his feet dangling in the water. Jinnah sits under an umbrella in an elegant white suit, being served tea by one of three or four servants around. Patel spews a fountain of water.

PATEL: I agree with Jinnah. Now that the Americans are in, the war will end soon. The Germans are worn out as it is . . . (*he rolls over, facing Nehru*) and our first act should be to convene a Congress Party convention and demand independence.

Nehru takes an iced drink from a servant.

JINNAH: And we must speak with one voice—united.

The others assent. Nehru shakes his head wistfully.

PATEL (*it reminds him*): Ah—we should invite Gandhi. What the devil has happened to him anyway?
NEHRU: He's "discovering" India.
JINNAH (*cynically*): Which is a lot better than causing trouble where it matters. Invite him—let him say his piece about South Africa—and then let him slip into oblivion.

Cut to

TRAIN. EXTERIOR. DAY.

A fireman heaps coal into an engine's boiler.
The train passes camera to the Third Class section, which seems besieged by humanity. People cling to the outside of each door and many more are seated on the central wooden planks on the roofs of the two coaches.

THIRD CLASS COACH. EXTERIOR. DAY.

Gandhi and Charlie are riding on the outside of the coach, hanging on through the door, and both enjoying it immensely. Ba, inside the jammed coach, finds it very unfunny. She has a grip on one of Gandhi's arms.

BA (*quietly, private*): Please! You're being foolish!

GANDHI: There's no room! And the air is lovely.

She grimaces severely and tugs at him.

CHARLIE: No violence, please.
GANDHI: Let me hang on with two hands or I will fall.

Featuring the roof. An Indian squats right on the edge of the roof above Charlie. He is looking down, offering a hand.

INDIAN (*over the sound of the engine*): Englishman Sahib!

Charlie, who has been grinning, suddenly looks baffled, not to say appalled.

INDIAN: Come! Come! There is room!

His hand still dangles in offering to the tall Charlie.
Another angle. Two other Indians on the roof move to where they can grip the first Indian's other arm, as counterforce to the weight of Charlie.

FIRST INDIAN (*to Charlie*): Place the foot on the window.

Featuring Charlie. Hesitatingly, he grips the inside of the window higher, and starts to swing one foot onto the window ledge.

GANDHI (*amused, but disconcerted*): What *are* you doing?
CHARLIE (*grimly*): Going nearer to God!

Gandhi, baffled a second, sees the outstretched hand above them, and in puckish complicity, helps boost Charlie up.
Long shot. As Charlie reaches up, his hand is grasped and he starts to scramble and be pulled up to the roof.
Featuring Gandhi and Ba. As Charlie's leg, assisted by Gandhi, starts to leave its lodging on the window ledge Ba suddenly turns, sees it, and grabs for it in alarm.

BA: Charlie! Be careful!!

Close shot. Charlie. His face flat on the roof of the train as his arm is still gripped by the Indian, but his leg is being pulled from behind.

CHARLIE (*desperately*): Mohan—!!

Resume Gandhi and Ba. Gandhi quickly moves to free

Ba's hand from Charlie's leg and almost loses his own grip. He grabs the window again.

GANDHI: Let go! You'll kill him!

Ba is confused.

GANDHI: Let go! Let go!

With one hand he pries at her grip. In the chaos of instructions others in the coach are helping Gandhi, and Ba senses she is doing something wrong, but is still not sure what. She lets go.
Close shot. Charlie. A desperate sigh of relief.
Long shot. Charlie is pulled on up to the top of the coach.
Featuring Charlie as he sits, puffing and recovering from the fright.

FIRST INDIAN: You see—most comfortable.

Charlie nods grimly.
Featuring Gandhi and Ba. Gandhi, smiling, goes on the tips of his toes to get a better view. Ba grabs him desperately.

BA: Please, God, no!

Featuring Charlie. He looks around at the rest of the passengers on the roof, their bundles and baskets clutched beside them. Their poverty is appalling, but they are all smiling at him, a sense of gaiety made in part by his Englishman's participation in their experience. They must shout over the train.

SECOND INDIAN (grinning): Are you Christian, Sahib?
CHARLIE (nods): Yes, yes, I'm a Christian.
SECOND INDIAN (proudly): I know a Christian. (Charlie acknowledges it politely.) She drinks blood.

Charlie stares at him in surprise.

SECOND INDIAN (explaining—obvious): The blood of Christ—every Sunday!

He is nodding, smiling, expecting Charlie's understanding. And Charlie gives it—somewhat bleakly. Suddenly

GANDHI'S VOICE *(alarmed)*: Charlie!!

The Indians turn. Charlie turns.

TRAIN AND TUNNEL. EXTERIOR. DAY.

Resume Charlie and the Indians.

FIRST INDIAN: It's all right, Sahib! Very safe—bend—bend!

All the Indians are crouching. Charlie closes his eyes ruefully—he's had better ideas than this—and he gets as flat as he can.

TRAIN AND TUNNEL. EXTERIOR. DAY.

The train, with passengers clinging to the sides and riding on the top, steams into the tunnel, its whistle sounding.

THE TUNNEL.

Black. A glimmer of light, through steam, the whistle echoing.

INDIAN'S VOICE: Pray to God, Sahib! Now is when it is best to be Hindu!

Close shot. Charlie. In a flash of steamy light, staring wide-eyed at the Indian.
Black, and sudden silence.
And we dissolve through to

CONVENTION TENT. INTERIOR. DAY.

High. Coming into focus is a lighted platform, and as the scene becomes clearer we see figures on the platform and the banner which reads INDIAN NATIONAL CONGRESS, and we hear the emotional voice of Jinnah at the microphone.

JINNAH *(gradually fading in)*: We were asked for toleration. We were asked for patience. Some gave it and some did not. Well, *their* war is over! And those of us who supported it, and those of us who refused must forget our differences!

The camera has been moving in; now it jumps to Jinnah

in close shot and intercuts with the impact of his fervid delivery on the audience.

JINNAH: And there can be no excuses from the British now! India wants Home Rule! India demands Home Rule!!

And the audience cheers him. Newspaper cameramen crowded around the platform photograph him. Patel comes forward from the back of the platform, clapping. He is chairing the Congress. Jinnah bows, taking his notes, gesturing to the auditorium. A man made for the spotlight, a man loving the spotlight.

At last he moves back to his place on the platform. Nehru clasps his hand in congratulation. Others crowd around him. And fleetingly, just in the edge of picture, we see Gandhi—again, the only one in an Indian tunic—sitting at the end of the second row on the platform. He is just watching the flood of enthusiasm for Jinnah.

Featuring Patel approaching the microphone, stilling the house with upraised hands.

PATEL: And let no one question that Mr. Jinnah speaks not just for the Muslims—but for all India!

And again the audience cheers and applauds his little coda. He raises his hands, stilling them again.

PATEL: And now I'm going to introduce to you a man whose writings we are all becoming familiar with . . . a man who stood high in the esteem of our beloved Gokhale . . . a man whose accomplishment in South Africa will always be remembered. Mr. Mohandas Gandhi.

Gandhi has already started to come toward the podium. He is greeted with mild applause, but already the convention is performing like a convention now that the spell of Jinnah's major speech has dissipated. As Gandhi reaches the podium, Patel gestures him to it.

PATEL (*politely*): Your journal has made a great impact.

Gandhi nods to him and acknowledges the residue of applause.

GANDHI: I am flattered by Mr. Patel. (*His grin.*) I would be even more flattered if what he said were true.

He means about the journal.

Patel has wandered back toward the others, his mind already on them. But he has half heard Gandhi's comment and turns—a smile, a politician's flexibility—

PATEL (*loudly; he is away from the mike*): But it's true! I—I read it . . . often.

Again Gandhi grins—and takes glasses from his sleeve. This is the first time we have seen them. He has one slip of paper with notes on it which he has put on the podium. He puts his glasses on and faces the convention.

GANDHI: Since I returned from South Africa, I have traveled over much of India. And I know I could travel many more years and still only see a small part of it.

On the platform, the whispered politics go on. On the floor of the convention, some listen, some talk of other things.

GANDHI: . . . and yet already I know what we say here means nothing to the masses of our country.

Nehru has turned, having caught that last remark. He touches Patel on the shoulder "Listen."

GANDHI: Here we make speeches for each other—and those English liberal magazines that may grant us a few lines.

And now they are beginning to pay attention on the floor of the hall too.

GANDHI: But the people of India are untouched. Their politics are confined to bread and salt.

Jinnah too is listening now—aloofly, challengingly.

GANDHI: Illiterate they may be, but they are not blind. They see no reason to give their loyalty to rich and powerful men who simply want to take over the role of the British in the name of freedom.

There is dissent on the floor and on the platform—but it is muttred and English "polite." Gandhi goes on.

GANDHI: This Congress tells the world it represents India. My brothers, India is seven hundred thousand "villages" not a few hundred lawyers in Delhi and Bombay. Until we stand in the fields with the millions who toil each day under the hot sun, we will not represent India—nor will we ever be able to challenge the British as one nation.

He takes off his glasses and folds them and in silence starts back toward his place on the platform. A cameraman flashes a picture, and someone begins to applaud; it is taken up here and there, tepidly. On the platform, the leaders join in perfunctorily. We see one peasant face (Shukla)—which we will come to know—watching from the crowd of outsiders who stand in the doorways.

Nehru, who has been looking at Gandhi with interest and some surprise turns to Patel.

NEHRU: Have you read his magazine?
PATEL: No—but I think I'm going to.

THE TRAIL TO GANDHI'S ASHRAM. EXTERIOR. DAY.

An open touring car struggling along the bumpy trail. Nehru drives, four friends as young as he with him, all dressed in the same expensive, British manner.

FIRST FRIEND: This can't be the way!

Nehru is looking a little harassed, from the ragging he is taking and from the ride. The ashram is only half-finished, the ground unworked, the buildings only partially completed and the whole looking like some primitive frontier outpost. They are finally brought to a halt by a goat that is tethered right across the path.

SECOND FRIEND (a mocking quote): Yes, I'm sure this is the direction India is taking.

The others laugh; Nehru suffers.

SECOND FRIEND: To think I almost got excited by Mr. Jinnah when all this was awaiting me.

ASHRAM. EXTERIOR. DAY.

Nehru has half risen in his seat to address Charlie Andrews, who, walking from one somnolent building to another, has stopped dead at the sight of the car. He carries sheaves of page proofs.

NEHRU: We're looking for Mr. Gandhi!

CHARLIE: Ah, you'll find him under the tree by the river. *(He points off, then glances at the car.)* You'd better leave the car—the ground is rather soft.

NEHRU: Thank you. . .

He looks around the ashram a little dismally.

FIRST FRIEND *(drolly, as he climbs out)*: Come on! I'm anxious to meet this new "force"!

ASHRAM. TREE BY RIVER. EXTERIOR. DAY.

Gandhi sits under a tree, peeling potatoes. Nehru and his friends are sprawled out around him. Beside them, the river; in the background the business of the ashram goes on.

GANDHI: I try to live like an Indian, as you see . . . it is stupid of course, because in our country it is the British who decide how an Indian lives—what he may buy, what he may sell. And from their luxury in the midst of our terrible poverty they instruct us on what is justice and what is sedition. *(He looks at them, a teasing but mordant grin.)* So it is only natural that our best young minds assume an air of Eastern dignity, while greedily assimilating every Western weakness as quickly a they can acquire it.

His smile is sardonic, but genuine, theirs embarrassed and self-conscious.

NEHRU *(defensively)*: If we have Home Rule that will change.

Gandhi has finished the last potato. He glances at Nehru then drops the potato in the bowl. He lifts the pail of peelings to Nehru.

GANDHI: Would you, please?

Nehru in his fine linen suit takes the pail awkwardly. His friends watch with amusement, but they too rise to follow as they head for the kitchen.

GANDHI: And why should the English grant us Home Rule? Here, we must take the peelings to the goats.

He re-directs Nehru toward a trough where two or three goats are tethered, but he keeps right on talking.

GANDHI: We only make wild speeches, or perform even wilder acts of terrorism. We've bred an army of anarchists but not one single group that can really fight the British anywhere.

NEHRU *(surprised)*: I thought you were against fighting.

They have reached the trough.

GANDHI: Just spread it around—they like the new peelings mixed with the rotting ones.

Nehru has carefully walked around something distasteful on the ground, now he dumps the peelings along the trough and spreads them "delicately." Gandhi scoops some peelings from the trough to feed a goat that nudges him.

GANDHI: Where there is injustice, I've always believed in fighting. *(He looks at Nehru.)* The question is do you fight to change things, or do you fight to punish. *(His smile.)* For myself, I have found that we are all such sinners we should leave punishment to God. And if we really want to change things there are better ways of doing it than by derailing trains or slashing someone with a sword.

He meets Nehru's gaze, and for a moment something deeper than argument passes between them. Then something catches Gandhi's eye. He looks off. Ba stands, watching him, waiting.

BA: The fire is ready.

Gandhi turns. The goat is reaching for his bowl of potatoes. He pushes it away and starts for the kitchen.

GANDHI: You see, even here we live under tyranny.

Nehru grins, captured by Gandhi's seriousness, and his humor. He hasn't moved, and neither have his friends. They watch Gandhi as he carries his bowl of potatoes to Ba.

NEHRU *(reflectively)*: I told you. . .

FIRST FRIEND: Hm . . . but look at him. Some "fighter"! I can see the British shaking now.

Gandhi plods on toward the kitchen, carrying the bowl of potatoes.

Gandhi (Ben Kingsley) as a young lawyer in South Africa receiving a vicious beating from a police sergeant (Ken Hutchinson). *Photo: Frank Connor.*

Mounted South African police charge marching Indian miners led by Gandhi. *Photo: Frank Connor.*

Gandhi and Khan (Amrish Puri) in jail for protesting South African Pass Laws. *Photo: Frank Connor.*

Charlie Andrews (Ian Charleson) visits Gandhi in jail at
Motihari, India. *Photo: Frank Connor.*

Gandhi's wife Ba (Rohini Hattangady) teaching her husband to use spinning wheel. *Photo: Frank Connor.*

Gandhi, after fast, supported by (left) Ba and Mirabehn (Geraldine James). *Photo: Frank Connor.*

Gandhi leading procession to beach at Dandi. *Photo: Frank Connor.*

Gandhi and salt marchers arrive at the sand dunes at Dandi. *Photo: Frank Connor.*

Walker (Martin Sheen) joining Gandhi at the head of the salt march.
Photo: Frank Connor.

Gandhi at Ba's deathbed. *Photo: Frank Connor.*

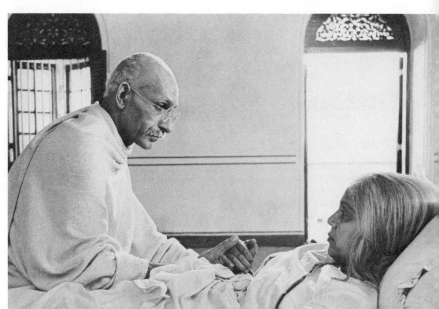

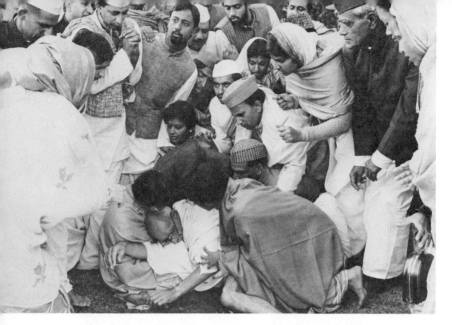

Gandhi is dead at the hand of an assassin. *Photo: Frank Connor.*

The Indian flag raised at the Red Fort, New Delhi.
Photo: Frank Connor.

THE RIVER BED AT THE ASHRAM. EXTERIOR. DAY.

Clothes are dipped in the brownish water. Ba and an ashramite woman squat by the river, washing clothes. It is long past the monsoons and they have had to come far out in the riverbed to the water. But they are laughing at their task.

BA: But it's the ink that is the most diffic—

She stops, because coming along the riverbed toward them is a man (Shukla) who looks as though he has come a long, weary way. His face is gaunt, his little bundle of belongings pathetic. As he nears them, he pauses.

SHUKLA: I am looking for Mr. Gandhi. . .

GANDHI'S HUT. ASHRAM. INTERIOR. DUSK.

Shadowed, the end of the day. Gandhi sits cross-legged, watching solemnly as Shukla reaches with his fingers into a bowl to eat. The fingers are thin, half-starved, like the man himself.

SHUKLA: . . . I've wanted to speak to you for a long time.

He looks up at Gandhi almost sheepishly. He does not eat yet, but his hunger is evident. Ba sits at one side in the shadows watching him as intently as Gandhi.

SHUKLA: . . . our crops . . . we can't sell them. . . We have no money . . . but the landlords take the same rent.

His voice is choked and near to tears, resonant with the unspoken agony his words mean for him and the others like him. He looks at Gandhi nervously for a moment, then puts the food to his mouth like a man who is starving, and trying desperately not to show it.

Close shot. Ba. The solemn intensity of her gaze reflects her identification with the man's agony. She glances up at Gandhi. . .

TRAIN STATION. CHAMPARAN. EXTERIOR. NIGHT.

The camera is low, shooting along the track toward the light of an approaching train. From its distant glow we can see that people line the platform of the small station, waiting, but we cannot tell how thick the crowd may be.

The station house. An open staff car pulls up through the press of the crowd. An English captain leaps out and pushes aggressively through the mass of bodies toward the platform. Again the darkness of the ill-lit station and the angle of the camera limit our vision.

ENGLISH CAPTAIN: Clear the way there! Get out of the way!

A detail of British troops, already on the station, moves in his wake, just as aggressive toward the crowd as he is.

SERGEANT PUTNAM: Sir! Up here!

The sergeant is on the low sloping roof of the station. The captain turns briskly to two of his detail.

ENGLISH CAPTAIN: Give me a leg up, will you!

The two men join hands and the captain is hoisted up with an assist from Sergeant Putnam. We hear the train stop in the background.

On the roof. The captain stands erect.

ENGLISH CAPTAIN: What the hell is it, Sergeant?

He is now standing and his face has frozen. It needs no answer from Putnam.

ENGLISH CAPTAIN: Jesus . . . !

He turns his head slowly, his mouth agape at

His point of view. The whole of the obscurely lit platform is covered thick with waiting crowds. They engulf the station house, back and front, and on the other side of the train more people are packed all along its length, and beyond them along the narrow street that stretches through the little collection of houses adjoining the station, every rooftop is covered—men, women with babes in arms, children. There is no excitement, hardly any movement—just a vast congregation of people, waiting silently in the darkness—and as the camera pans we see that the crowd extends, indiscernible, even beyond the range of light.

ENGLISH CAPTAIN (*awed, a little frightened*): What the hell is going on?

SERGEANT PUTNAM: I don't know, sir. The agent says they got a telegram and it just said, he is coming . . . and gave the time of the train.

ENGLISH CAPTAIN: Who the hell is *he?*

SERGEANT PUTNAM: I don't know, sir.

Featuring Gandhi. He has stepped down from the train. Shukla guides him, Ba and Charlie a step or two behind. Gandhi moves through the silent crowd, his hands in the *pranam*, bowing a little to either side. As he advances, the crowd parts—it is almost eerily silent. As their clothes indicate, the area is Muslim, so some salaam (a touch of the hand to the forehead) and a few tentatively make the *pranam* back to Gandhi as he moves through them. Most of the faces are gaunt and lean. A destitute people.

And suddenly there is a commotion and the sound of boots on the concrete platform, and the English captain shoves his way through to confront Gandhi down the little aisle that was being made for him. The sergeant and part of the detail are behind the captain.

The captain stares. Then he looks around at the crowd, suspiciously, a touch of inner fear, then back to Gandhi.

ENGLISH CAPTAIN: Who the devil are you?

GANDHI: My name is Gandhi. Mohandas K. Gandhi.

There is a flicker of recognition, but uncertain. The captain stiffens; a steeling of the will. Another glance at the crowd, this time with an air of outraged authority.

ENGLISH CAPTAIN: Well, whoever you are, we don't want you here. I suggest you get back on that train before it leaves the station.

GANDHI (*calmly, a glance at the crowd*): *They* seem to want me.

ENGLISH CAPTAIN: Now look here. I'll put you under arrest if you'd prefer!

GANDHI: On what charge?

It has the cold assurance of a lawyer, and the Captain is a little shaken by it. He glances at Charlie who stands behind Gandhi now, and it makes him all the more uncertain.

ENGLISH CAPTAIN: I don't want any trouble.

He tries to make it severe, but it is a comedown.

GANDHI: I am an Indian traveling in my own country. I see no reason for trouble.

It is firm and there is an edge of assertiveness to it that the Captain doesn't like, but Gandhi's unrelenting stare unnerves him. He glances at Charlie again.

ENGLISH CAPTAIN: Well, there'd better not be.

Again, the empty severity of weakness. He looks around, then turns and marches off briskly shoving his way through the crowd. "Out of my way, there! Come on, move!"
Gandhi smiles reflectively, and the crowd suddenly begins to buzz. Where all was silence before there is now the hum of excitement. Already he has scored a victory—and as he moves forward again, making the *pranam*, they return it with flushed greetings. "Gandhi—Gandhi—Bapu—Gandhiji" . . .

A PEASANT'S DWELLING. INTERIOR. DAY.

The early light of the sun illumines the dwelling. We feature a man in middle age, but one who looks ill and drawn (Meha). He lies on a straw mat.

MEHA: For years the landlords have ordered us to grow indigo, for dyeing the cloth. Always they took part of the crop as rent.

Gandhi sits cross-legged, listening. It is the kind of listening that opens the heart. Behind him a mass of villagers sits stoically, outside the dwelling, waiting while their case is heard. Meha tries to speak unemotionally but under Gandhi's sympathetic gaze his despair keeps cracking through.

MEHA: But now the English factories make cloth for everyone. No one wants our indigo. And the landlords won't take their share. They say we must pay our rent in cash.

Near to breakdown, he gestures around the empty house.

MEHA: What we could, we sold. . . . The police have taken the rest. There is no food, we—

He cannot go on.

GANDHI: I understand. *(He examines his hands a moment.)* The landlords are British?

It's a rhetorical question. Meha nods.

Gandhi looks around the crude dwelling, almost nothing remains. We see two young men, one seventeen perhaps, the other older, and a girl, sixteen. And finally Meha's wife, sitting near Ba, the two women listening together but Meha's wife looks like a woman who has given up, her hair is dead and hardly combed, her sari dirty.

Meha looks at Gandhi and shakes his head hopelessly. Gandhi nods. . . He stands slowly.

GANDHI: What we can do . . . we will try to do.

The words are said bleakly, not to raise false hopes. He glances at Meha's wife. Water comes to her eyes, and she lowers her head. Ba puts her hands on her shoulders and clasps her to her, and the woman breaks, and sobs and sobs. . .

TILLED FIELD. CHAMPARAN. EXTERIOR. DAY.

Gandhi rides on an open howdah on an elephant, his mind locked in somber reflection. Shukla shares the howdah with him, but does not dare break Gandhi's black mood.

GANDHI: Is all Champaran like this, Shukla?
SHUKLA: Yes, Bapu . . . *(He looks across the field.)* The whole province . . . hundreds—thousands.

It registers with Gandhi—but inside. A moment.

CHARLIE'S VOICE: Mohan—!

Gandhi shakes himself from his absorption and looks back. Ba and Charlie are mounted on a similar howdah on another elephant, both being led by peasant boys. Charlie is pointing behind them. Coming along the path is a tall Indian policeman on a bicycle. He rides right past Charlie and Ba and comes alongside Gandhi. His attitude is superficially polite, but he is full of righteous authority.

POLICEMAN *(he knows)*: Are you Mr. M. K. Gandhi?
GANDHI: Yes.

POLICEMAN: I'm sorry but you are under arrest.
GANDHI: I am not sorry at all.

It contains more anger than we have seen him display to anyone but Ba.

CHAMPARAN CRICKET CLUB. EXTERIOR. DAY.

A ball is hit. The camera pulls back to reveal a lush, verdant pitch, white-garbed players, English, a few ladies dressed in First World War fashion watching under parasols near the clubhouse and in the shade of trees with a few officers and civil servants, while Indian servants discreetly serve cool drinks.

The batsman has hit a four and we see him run down the pitch with his partner until the four is certain, then

BATSMAN (*to the wicket keeper*): Who did you say would be buying the drinks?

The wicket keeper makes a rude, facetious gesture, but as the batsman turns to settle in his crease again

BATSMAN: Oh, no—

He has looked up. A car is pulling hurriedly in near the clubhouse, an officer in it, and people are streaming toward it.

The car. A major is standing on the back seat. An Indian corporal drives.

MAJOR: . . . I've got no idea. All I know is there's a riot or some- thing at Motihari in Champaran, and the whole company is ordered out.
A VOICE: It's two days' march!
MAJOR: That's why the match is off. It's mostly Muslim territory and the old man's taking no chances.

Feturing the batsman and some of the players as they walk across the field toward the car. They know something's up

BATSMAN (*disgusted*): God, and it's the best innings I've had since Oxford.

WICKET KEEPER (drily): India's full of grief, old man.

The batsman "takes" on him facetiously, and we cut to

THE COURTHOUSE AND JAIL. MOTIHARI.
EXTERIOR. DAY.

A small building on a little Anglicized square. It is surrounded by a milling angry throng of peasants.

Featuring the front entrance. The English captain who was at the station when Gandhi arrived is on the top step, looking harried and tense. A small detachment of Indian troops lines the step below him. Charlie Andrews is pushing through the crowd toward the captain. As he approaches, the Indian sergeant holds up his hand.

CHARLIE (firmly): I wish to see the prisoner, please.

The captain looks at his clerical collar, his English face, his determination.

CAPTAIN (reluctantly): All right, Sergeant.

Charlie moves through the Indian soldiers and up toward the entrance. The captain stares out worriedly over the unruly crowd.

COURTHOUSE JAIL. INTERIOR. DAY.

A basement chamber—dark, thick-walled and poorly lit. The camera has panned off a close shot of Gandhi as he turns in his cell at the sound of a door opening and approaching footsteps. We have seen only his head and shoulders, which are covered in a shawl.

A police guard leads Charlie across the rough, unfinished floor. As he comes to Gandhi's cell we get a fleeting glimpse of Gandhi sitting on a low pallet bed.

Close shot. Gandhi as he recognizes his visitor.

GANDHI: Charlie—

Reverse on Charlie. He looks down at Gandhi and shakes his head.

CHARLIE (*a somber grin*): . . . Shades of South Africa.

Close shot. Gandhi. Head and shoulders. He returns the grin, but anger and determination still dominate his mood.

GANDHI: Not quite. They're only "holding me" until the Magistrate's hearing. Then it will be prison.

CHARLIE (*sympathetically*): Did they take your cothes?

And now we see Gandhi in full shot for the first time. He is wearing only a white loincloth, the shawl over his shoulders and sandals—the costume he will wear for the rest of his life.

GANDHI: These are my clothes now.

Charlie studies him a moment, and being Charlie, he understands.

CHARLIE (*affectionately*): You always had a puritanical streak. Mohan.

He grins, and it elicits a little grin from Gandhi.

GANDHI (*in a tone of defensiveness*): If I want to be one with them, I have to live like them.

CHARLIE: I think you do. (*A smile.*) But I thank God we all don't.

And Gandhi laughs.

GANDHI: I'm sure your legs are quite as handsome as mine.

CHARLIE: Ah, but my puritanism runs another way. I'm far too modest for such a display.

And again Gandhi laughs. Charlie turns to the guard.

CHARLIE: Couldn't I be let in with the prisoner? I am a clergyman.

The police guard hesitates, and then unlocks the cell.
Charlie enters and sits on a little wooden stool opposite Gandhi, his long legs awkwardly filling most of the space between them. Gandhi has remained seated, pensive. Charlie studies him a moment.

CHARLIE (*a bit puzzled*): They're calling you "Bapu." I thought it meant father.

GANDHI (*wistfully*): It does. We must be getting old, Charlie.

A little grin, but his mood remains pensive—and remote.

CHARLIE: What do you want me to do?

Gandhi looks up—his anger, his determination there, but then broken by a hopeless sigh.

GANDHI: I think, Charlie, that you can help us most by taking that assignment you've been offered in Fiji.

Charlie is stunned, and obviously hurt. Gandhi proceeds more gently.

GANDHI: I have to be sure—they have to be sure—that what we do can be done by Indians . . . alone.

And now Charlie understands. Gandhi smiles; warmth, and sadness. Then he speaks with a determined purposeful-ness, a friend's trust.

GANDHI: But you know the strategy. The world is full of people who will despise what's happening here. It is their strength we need. Before you go, you could start us in the right direction.

He has taken some scrawled notes from under the bed-ding and handed them to Charlie. Charlie nods. He sighs, and rises slowly.

CHARLIE: I must leave from Calcutta, and soon. You'll have to say goodbye to Ba for me.

Gandhi rises, glancing wryly at the prison walls. He nods.

GANDHI: When I get the chance.

And now he faces Charlie; this is the moment of farewell.

CHARLIE: Well, I—

He doesn't know what to say, how to say it. Gandhi meets his eyes—a smile that shelters Charlie's vulnerability, returns his love.

GANDHI: There are no goodbyes for us, Charlie. Wherever you are, you will always be in my heart. . .

The very English, very steadfast Charlie fights to contain his emotions.

THE COURTROOM. MOTIHARI. INTERIOR. DAY.

It is packed to overflowing; restless. Gandhi sits in the dock. One or two sergeants-at-arms are trying to keep order, but it is the uneven and menacing chanting of "Gandhi . . . Gandhi" coming from the mobs outside the courtroom that fills the atmosphere with threat.

The magistrate (English) is surveying the courtroom; he signals his clerk (English) to him.

MAGISTRATE *(whispered conference)*: I am going to clear the courtroom.

CLERK *(politely)*: I'm not sure we'd be able to. And it is a first hearing, it's supposed to be public. And he's a lawyer.

The magistrate frowns.

MAGISTRATE *(worried, angry)*: I don't know where they found the nerve for all this.

CLERK: I'm sure I don't either, but the troops won't be here until tomorrow.

MAGISTRATE: How did the press get here before the military?

We see the front row from his point of view. Two or three Indian journalists and one European.

CLERK: That English clergyman sent a number of telegrams yesterday afternoon. I understand one of them even went to the Viceroy.

The magistrate receives that news with some alarm. He indicates that the clerk take his place.

Gandhi stands. The courtroom is silent, but we can still hear the sound of the chanting outside.

MAGISTRATE: You have been ordered out of the province on the grounds of disturbing the peace.

GANDHI *(defiantly)*: With respect, I refuse to go.

The magistrate stares. The journalists write. The clerk swallows.

The magistrate looks around the courtroom and is only too aware of the mob outside.

MAGISTRATE *(sternly)*: Do you want to go to jail?

GANDHI (*not giving him an inch*): As you wish.

The clerk lowers his eyes to his pad. The magistrate searches the distant wall, the top of his desk, his twitching hands for an answer. Finally

MAGISTRATE (*as much sternness as he can muster*): All right. I will release you on bail of one hundred rupees until I reach a sentence.

GANDHI: I refuse to pay one hundred rupees.

Again the magistrate stares. And so do the journalists. The magistrate wets his lips—

MAGISTRATE: Then I—I will grant release without bail—until I reach a decision.

And now the court explodes. In the chaos of cheering and delight, the magistrate rises, looks around the room and heads for his chambers.

The journalists are scribbling furiously.

Gandhi turns and starts outof the courtroom. We hear cries of "Gandhi!—Gandhi!—Bapu!"

THE COURTHOUSE BALCONY.

Gandhi steps from the courtroom to the balcony. A huge cheer comes up from the massed peasants below. As he smiles down at them, he is turned by

A VOICE: Gandhiji!—Gandhiji! Mr. Gandhi!

Four young Indians—elegantly dressed in English clothes —are following him, having plunged through the crowd in the courtroom. A beat—and the first young man addresses him over the chaos.

FIRST YOUNG MAN (*his accent is as refined as his clothes*): Gandhiji—we are from Bihar. We received a cable this morning from an old friend who was at Cambridge with us. (*A smile.*) His name is Nehru and I believe you know him.

Gandhi reacts—with surprise and caution.

GANDHI: Indeed.

FIRST YOUNG MAN: He tells us you need help. And we have come to give it.

Again Gandhi is surprised—but even more cautious. Behind him, the crowd begins to chant "Gandhi—Gandhi."

GANDHI: I want to document, coldly, rationally, what is being done here. It may take months—many, many months.

FIRST YOUNG MAN (*they're eager, impressed*): We have no pressing engagements.

It sounds casually ironic, but they look determined, even angry.

GANDHI: You will have to live with the peasants. (*They nod.*) I have nothing to pay you. (*They only smile.*) Hmm.

He is looking at them with a soupçon of scepticism but he is beginning to smell victory. His name echoes around him and is taken up even louder as the news spreads to the street.

GOVERNOR'S OFFICE. CHAMPARAN. INTERIOR. DAY.

Almost total silence. The room is long, large and imposing—hardwood floors, overhead fans, an aura of wealth and permanence. Footsteps pace its acres of space . . . and Sir George Hodge comes into frame. He is rich, middle-aged, Tory—and at the moment feeling impotent and harried.

SIR GEORGE: I don't know what this country is coming to!

The Governor, Sir Edward Gait—the portrait of the King prominent behind him—is feeling as cornered as Sir George but for different reasons. His desk is arrayed with several tall stacks of folders—all with exactly the same-covers—and on one corner of the desk, some folded newspapers. We can just read "Gandhi" in a headline. He taps one of the folders irritably with his hand.

SIR EDWARD: But good God, man, you yourself raised the rent simply to finance a hunting expedition!

Sir George looks at him—half defensive, half defiant.

They are old friends—the same school, the same social class, long together in India—and their argument is an argument between friends who accept the same premises. But even so the Governor feels the game has not quite been played fairly.

SIR EDWARD: And some of these others—*(he gestures to the folders again)* beatings, illegal seizures, demanding services without pay, even refusing them water! In India! . . .

Sir George is staring out of the window, vexed, bristling but defensive.

SIR GEORGE: Nobody knows what it is to try to get these people to work!

SIR EDWARD: Well, you've made this half-naked whatever-he-is into an international hero.

He picks up one of the papers irritatedly, the *London Daily Chronicle*.

SIR EDWARD: "One lone man marching dusty roads armed only with honesty and a bamboo shaft doing battle with the British Empire." *(He lowers the paper dismally; then the ultimate bitterness)* At home children are writing "essays" about him.

Sir George looks at him and sighs heavily. Sir Edward stares back, then drops the paper back on his desk.

SIR EDWARD: I couldn't take another two years of him to save my life.

Sir George turns, and paces back toward him. For the first time we see Sir Edward's personal secretary (a male civil servant) sitting at a small desk and listening with highly developed unobtrusiveness.

SIR GEORGE: What do they want?

It is the first sign of concession. Sir Edward lifts his eyes to his personal secretary.

PERSONAL SECRETARY *(reading precisely from a document)*: A rebate on rents paid. *(Sir George huffs.)* They are to be free to grow crops of their own choice. A commission—part *Indian*—to hear grievances.

Sir George looks from him to Sir Edward. A beat.

SIR GEORGE *(wearily)*: That would satisfy him? . . .

SIR EDWARD *(a nod; then pointedly)*: *And* His Majesty's Government. It only needs your signature for the landlords.

Sir George looks at the document on the secretary's desk. A moment. The secretary turns it slowly so it is facing him. Sir George looks at it like a snake. The secretary picks up a pen and offers it. A second, then Sir George takes the pen and signs angrily.

SIR GEORGE: It will be worth it to see the back of him. *(A flourish at the end of his signature, then he stands.)* We're too damn liberal.

Sir Edward is at the liquor cabinet.

SIR EDWARD: Perhaps. But at least all this has made the Government see some sense about what men like Mr. Gandhi should be allowed, and what they should be denied.

He turns, offering Sir George a whiskey in a finely cut glass of crystal.

SIR EDWARD *(firmly)*: Things are going to change.

JINNAH'S RESIDENCE. BOMBAY. EXTERIOR. DAY.

Jinnah moves from under the portico. His shining, expensive car is coming in the drive and stops by him. He opens the back door, but only the chauffeur is in the car.

JINNAH *(in annoyance)*: Where is Mr. Gandhi?

CHAUFFEUR *(distastefully)*: He said he preferred to walk, sir. I followed him most of the way. He's just turned the corner.

Jinnah closes the door and looks across at the entrance in exasperation.

JINNAH: The Prophet give me patience.

CHAUFFEUR: He came Third Class.

It's a disdainful comment and he drives the car off toward the garage.

Gandhi comes around the corner of the wall into the entrance. He is carrying a bedroll and a bamboo walking stick. Herman Kallenbach is with him, dressed informally, also carrying a bedroll. Jinnah makes a "sophisticated" salaam.

JINNAH *(with effort)*: My house is honored.

Gandhi grins, dismissing the formality.

GANDHI *(he makes the* pranam)*:* The honor is ours. May I introduce Mr. Kallenbach. He's an old friend *(anticipating Jinnah's objection)* and his interest is in flowers. I presumed to tell him he could wander your gardens while we talked.

JINNAH *(the suave, but slightly ironic host)*: I'll send my gardener. I'm sure you'll have much to discuss.

JINNAH'S DRAWING ROOM. INTERIOR. DAY.

It is spacious, "English." At the door, Jinnah introduces Gandhi to the room.

JINNAH: Gentlemen—the hero of Champaran.

Again Gandhi grins at the extravagance.

GANDHI: Only the stubborn man of Champaran.

A polite little laugh; Jinnah introduces him.

JINNAH: Mr. Patel you know. *(Patel bows.)* Mr. Maulana Azad—a fellow Muslim . . . recently released from prison.

Gandhi makes the *pranam*, studying him with interest after that comment. Azad gives a gentle salaam.

JINNAH: Mr. Kripalani. *(A bow—we have seen him at the Congress Conference.)* And of course you know Mr. Nehru.

Gandhi turns.
Featuring Nehru. He stands, awaiting Gandhi's attention. All the others have been dressed in European clothes. The handsome Europeanized Nehru now wears an Indian tunic—much like the one that Gandhi once wore.
For a moment Gandhi studies the costume, then a broad smile.

GANDHI *(a play on Jinnah's introduction)*: I am *beginning* to know Mr. Nehru.

PATEL (*to business: Gandhi has been admitted to the power circle, he is not the power*): Well, I've called you here because I've had a chance to see the new legislation. It's exactly what was rumored. Arrest without warrant. Automatic imprisonment for possession of materials considered seditious . . .

He looks at Gandhi.

PATEL: Your writings are specifically listed.

Gandhi nods at the "compliment," but they are all angered by the severity of it.

KRIPALANI: So much for helping them in the Great War . . .

JINNAH (*fire*): There is only one answer to that. Direct action—on a scale they can never handle!

Again the temper of it produces a little silence. Then

NEHRU: I don't think so.

He moves to a servant who stands, holding a large tray with a silver service of tea. Of them all, Nehru's manner is the most naturally patrician and Jinnah watches him with a somewhat envious awareness of it.

NEHRU: Terrorism would only justify their repression. And what kinds of leaders would it throw up? Are they likely to be the men we would want at the head of our country?

His stand has produced a little shock of surprise. Holding his tea, he turns to Gandhi with a little smile.

NEHRU: I've been catching up on my reading.

He means Gandhi's of course. Jinnah looks at the two of them. Gandhi has removed his sandals and is sitting cross-legged on a fine upholstered chair. Jinnah's eyes rake him with anger and distaste.

JINNAH (*coldly*): I too have read Mr. Gandhi's writtings, but I'd rather be ruled by an Indian terrorist than an English one. And I don't want to submit to that kind of law.

PATEL (*to Nehru—diplomatically—but with a trace of condescension*): I must say, Panditji, it seems to me it's gone beyond remedies like passive resistance.

GANDHI (*in the silence*): If I may—I, for one, have never advocated passive anything.

They all look at him with some surprise. As he speaks, he rises and walks to the servant.

GANDHI: I am with Mr. Jinnah. We must never submit to such laws—ever. And I think our resistance must be active and provocative.

They all stare at him, startled by his words and the fervor with which he speaks to them.

GANDHI: I want to embarrass all those who wish to treat us as slaves. All of them.

He holds their gaze, then turns to the immobile servant and with a little smile, takes the tray from him and places it on the table next to him. It makes them all aware that the servant, standing there like an insensate ornament, has been treated like a "thing," a slave. As it sinks in, Gandhi pours some tea then looks up at them with a pleading warmth—first to Jinnah.

GANDHI: Forgive my stupid illustration. But I want to change their *minds*—not kill them for weaknesses we all possess.

It impresses each one of them. But for all his impact, they still take the measure of him with caution.

AZAD: And what "resistance" would you offer?
GANDHI: The law is due to take effect from April sixth. I want to call on the nation to make that a day of prayer and fasting.

"Prayer and fasting"? They are not overwhelmed.

JINNAH: You mean a general strike?
GANDHI *(his grin)*: I mean a day of prayer and fasting. But of course no work could be done—no buses, no trains, no factories, no administration. The country would stop.

Patel is the first to recognize the implications.

PATEL: My God, it would terrify them . . .
AZAD *(a wry smile)*: Three hundred fifty million people at prayer. Even the English newspapers would have to report *that*. And explain why.
KRIPALANI: But could we get people to do it?
NEHRU *(he is half sold already)*: Champaran stirred the whole country. *(To Gandhi)* They are calling you Mahatma—the Great Soul.

GANDHI: Fortunately such news comes very slowly where I live.
NEHRU (*continuing, to the others*): I think if we all worked to publicize it . . . all of the Congress . . . every avenue we know.

The idea has caught hold. As the others talk of "papers," "telegrams," "speeches," Jinnah looks over his cup at Gandhi with an air of bitter resignation, but he tries to make light of it.

JINNAH: Perhaps I should have stayed in the garden and talked about the flowers.

THE GARDEN. VICEROY'S PALACE. EXTERIOR. DAY.

A garden party in full imperial splendor. A military band plays discreetly in the background. Princes, maharajahs, generals, ranking British civil servants and their ladies taking tea on the manicured lawns among the exotic flowers. But over all there is a thread of anxiety, we pick up one or two nervous phrases: "At the West Gate there were no taxis at all!," "Of course, the Army will always be loyal." And the camera picks out a civil servant stepping from a door of the palace carrying a sheaf of telegrams and cable forms.

He searches the assembled guests, then heads with almost indecorous haste toward his target. It is the Viceroy, Lord Chelmsford. With him, talking quietly, are his aide-de-camp, the Governor of the province and his ADC, and the commanding general of the Army in India. Lord Chelmsford's ADC is the first to react to the civil servant's arrival and his impatient attendance.

ADC: Sir—it's Mr. Kinnoch.

Lord Chelmsford turns expectantly.

CHELMSFORD: Yes?
KINNOCH (*hesitant, stunned*): Nothing . . . nothing is working, sir—buses . . . trains . . . the markets . . . (*Personal, incredulous*) There's not even any civilian staff here, sir. . . Everything has stopped.
CHELMSFORD (*curt, firm*): Is it simply Delhi and Bombay?

His firmness doesn't restore Kinnoch's normal aplomb. He holds the telegrams forward.

KINNOCH: No, sir—Karachi, Calcutta, Madras, Bangalore. It's, it's total.

He glances at the general.

KINNOCH *(the ultimate)*: The Army had to take over the telegraph or we'd be cut off from the world.

That takes the wind out of all of them. Grimly, Lord Chelmsford looks out across the palace's ordered lawns and gardens.

CHELMSFORD: I can't believe it. . .

KINNOCH: He's going to sell his own paper tomorrow in Bombay. They've called for a parade—on Victoria Road.

CHELMSFORD *(clenches his jaw and turns to the General)*: Arrest him!

THE JAIL. BOMBAY. INTERIOR. DAY.

A prison door opens. Gandhi, in prison clothes, is led along a small corridor to a room. The door is held open by a prison guard.

A ROOM. THE JAIL. BOMBAY. INTERIOR. DAY.

Nehru waits for Gandhi. He rises when Gandhi enters. The guard signals Gandhi to a chair across a small wooden table from Nehru. The guard closes the door, but remains in the room. Nehru's face is a map of concern, but he manages a small smile of greeting.

NEHRU: Bapu . . .

Gandhi, who also looks worn, raises his eyebrows whimsically at the use of that name.

GANDHI: You too . . .

He means "Bapu"—"Father."

NEHRU *(a real smile, but the same affection)*: It seems less formal than "Mahatma."

Gandhi sighs, and their faces and minds go to more somber matters.

NEHRU: Since your arrest the riots have hardly stopped. Not big— but they keep breaking out. I run to stop them . . . and Patel and Kripalani—they are never at rest. But some English civil- ians have been killed, and the Army is attacking crowds with clubs—and sometimes worse.

Gandhi has listened to it all with a growing sense of despair.

GANDHI: Maybe I'm wrong . . . maybe we're not ready yet. In South Africa the numbers were small. . .

NEHRU: The Government's afraid, and they don't know what to do. But they're more afraid of terrorists than of you. The Viceroy has agreed to your release if you will speak for non- violence.

GANDHI (*a sad smile*): I've never spoken for anything else.

THE STREETS OF AMRITSAR. EXTERIOR. DAY.

The golden dome of the Temple fills the screen, shim- mering. The sound of a car, and marching feet. The camera pulls back from the dome, revealing the rooftops, the trees and then suddenly, center of frame, the face of General Dyer—blunt, cold, isolated in a cocoon of vengeful military righteousness. He is traveling slowly, steadily in an armored car at the head of fifty armed sepoys—Gurkhas and Bal- uchis—immaculate, precise, awesome. Behind them a staff car with Dyer's English ADC and a British police officer. It is a relentless, determined procession, filling the dusty street with a sense of menace and foreboding.

JALLIANWALLAH BAGH. AMRITSAR.
EXTERIOR. DAY.

A large public garden, enclosed by a thick, old, crumbling wall. A large crowd is gathered around a speaker on a plat- form at one side of the park. It is political, but the crowd is mixed. We see Muslims and Hindus, many of them Sikhs, old men, little children, women with babes in arms. Some donkey carts, a sense of fair-time gaiety.

We close in on the speaker—a Muslim. He clutches a copy (we need not see the title) of Gandhi's journal.

SPEAKER: . . . England is so powerful—its army and its navy, all its modern weapons—but when a great power like that strikes defenseless people it shows its brutality, its own weakness! Especially when those people do not strike back. *(He holds aloft the clenched journal.)* That is why the Mahatma begs us to take the course of nonviolence!

THE ENTRANCE OF THE JALLIANWALLAH BAGH. EXTERIOR. DAY.

General Dyer, his armored car, his sepoys, moving toward the gate. Dyer looks ahead calmly.

His point of view. The Gate of the Bagh. A rickety double gate in the high crumbling wall. On each pillar, poster notices for the meeting: "For Congress—For Gandhi." In the distance the speaker and the assembled crowd. Nearer, a few vendors, loiterers and children. At the sound of the armoured car and marching feet, a few turn in curiosity.

Another angle. The armored car grinds forward. It won't go through the gates, one fender scraping against the gate post. Dyer gives a quiet order, the car backs away. Dyer jumps down lightly—a man in splendid condition. He walks through the gate and stands quietly in the at-ease position, hands clasping his swagger stick behind his back, looking off at

The speaker—medium shot.

SPEAKER: . . . If we riot, if we fight back, *we* become the vandals and they become the law! If we bear their blows, *they* are the vandals—God and His law are on our . . . *(He glances up.)* side.

Long shot—his point of view. The two platoons of sepoys, rifles at the port, trot smartly through the gate and fan out on either side of the motionless and dominant figure of Dyer.

Resume the speaker.

SPEAKER *(soldiering on)*: . . . We must have the courage to take their anger . . .

Medium close—the sepoys and Dyer. He issues his commands in a quiet and unemotional voice, as though they were on maneuvers.

DYER: Port arms, Sergeant Major.

The sergeant major issues the command. The troops port arms.

DYER: Load.

Again, the sergeant major barks the command, the bolts slam back and forth, the magazines clatter.

Featuring the platform and the front of the crowd. They have all turned now to watch, frozen in incredulity and fascination. The sound of the sergeant major's orders and the sinister rattle of breeches and bolts drifting to them.

SPEAKER (*almost to himself as he too is riveted*): . . . Our pain will be our victory.

Their point of view. The distant figures facing them.

Resume the crowd. Numbly they begin to back away, pressing against the speaker's stand, themselves. A man picks up a child.

Their point of view. The small, distant figures of the sepoys again. A word of command. One platoon kneels and takes aim. Another command. The second platoon, standing behind the first, takes aim.

Featuring Dyer. His ADC approaches. The British police officer stands off to one side.

ADC: Do we issue a warning, sir?
DYER (*stiffly*): They've had their warning—no meetings.

It is final.

Resume the crowd. A ripple of panic now, everyone pressing back, but still they cannot credit what they see. Only one or two have the presence of mind to push clear and seek shelter. It is too late.

Close shot Dyer, still calm.

DYER: Sergeant Major—
SERGEANT MAJOR: Take aim!

Long shot over the sepoys and their sights, the wavering crowd distant.

DYER: Fire!

Flash shot along the line of sepoys; the rifles jerk and bang. The crowd, running, screaming.

SERGEANT MAJOR: Reload!

A dreadful press of panic-stricken people flying toward the walls. And again the crash of rifles. Some fall. Others run off-screen in an aimless, irresistible wave.

Dyer is walking behind his men, telling them, with a view to maximum accuracy, what he has told them on the firing range (it makes him a little irritable to have to repeat it).

DYER: Take your time. Take your time.

He looks off at the crowd. His eyes narrow.

A group of men are hurling themselves at a breach in the top of the wall, hanging there, scrabbling for a purchase, some disappearing, a few heroic individuals astride the wall reaching down to assist their women and children in the swirling crowd below.

DYER: Corporal!
CORPORAL: Sir!
DYER: Over there.

He nods. The corporal looks.

CORPORAL: Sir.

He directs the attention of his neighbors in the firing line toward the new target; they shift their aim.

A man reaching for a child—who is also propelled upward by its mother from below—is hit, falls, so that he and the child crash into the crowd below.

Sepoys firing ad lib. Dyer watching the effect, careful and conscientious.

Swift tracking a man running through the staggering crowd, over the litter of bodies, his mouth open, his eyes wild. He arrives at a well, throws down the rope and slides down it. Others seize the idea and in panic throw themselves into the well, dropping out of sight.

Featuring Dyer. Meticulously, he taps a corporal on the shoulder with his swagger stick and indicates the well. The corporal signals his line of men.

At the well. The gathering crowd—men, women—and laced with rifle fire.

From behind the sepoys we see the whole Bagh, littered with dead and dying, a thick ruck around the well, the walls hanging with wounded and dying, the firing continuing, loud, loud, louder . . . until—

Cut to

THE ARMORY HALL. THE FORT OF LAHORE. INTERIOR. DAY.

Silence. The camera is close as it crosses a table with legal documents. Gradually we hear a muffled cough, whispers, shuffled papers, and it at last comes to a large close shot of General Dyer.

Another angle. A Commission of Inquiry sits in the large Armory Hall of th Old Fort. Dyer faces a panel of Commissioners: Lord Hunter, presiding, Mr. Justice Rankin, General Barrow, a British civil servant, and an Indian barrister.

The Commission functions like a public parliamentary committee—little ceremony, no judicial robes, a small group of public and press, who sit on wooden chairs behind a barrier that isolates the Commission's business.

Much of that public is English—fellow officers and civilians.

A Government Advocate (English) turns to face Dyer.

ADVOCATE: General Dyer, is it correct that you ordered your troops to fire at the thickest part of the crowd?

Dyer glances woodenly at the panel—a man in some shock at the consequences of what he assumed was an act worthy of praise.

DYER (*righteously*): That is so.

The Advocate looks at him with a degree of disbelief—more at his attitude than his statement.

ADVOCATE: One thousand five hundred and sixteen casualties with one thousand six hundred and fifty bullets.

A slight reaction from the public section. Dyer's jaw tightens.

DYER: My intention was to inflict a lesson that would have an impact throughout all India.

He stares at the panel like a reasonable man making a reasonable point. The evasiveness, the only half-buried embarrassment of their response only deepens his own withdrawal into himself.

INDIAN BARRISTER: General, had you been able to take in the armored car, would you have opened fire with the machine gun?

Dyer thinks about it. Then unashamedly—

DYER: I think, probably—yes.

A muted reaction from the public section. The Indian barrister stares at him a moment, then simply lowers his eyes to his notes.

HUNTER: General, did you realize there were children—and women—in the crowd?
DYER (*a beat*): I did.

For the first time there is the hint of uncertainty in his manner.

ADVOCATE: But that was irrelevant to the point you were making?
DYER: That is correct.

There is just a tremor of distaste quickly suppressed among the panel. Not so quickly in the public section.

ADVOCATE: Could I ask you what provision you made for the wounded?

Dyer looks at him quickly. The question is unexpected, even a little "clever." The officers listening clearly resent it.

DYER (*a moment, then firmly*): I was ready to help any who applied.

And that answer stops the Advocate. He smiles dryly.

ADVOCATE: General . . . how does a child shot with a 3-0-3 Enfield "apply" for help?

Dyer faces him stonily, a seed of panic taking root deep in his gut.

JALLIANWALLAH BAGH. EXTERIOR. DAY.

Quiet: the same silence as at the Court of Inquiry. The camera is panning slowly along a section of the wall. We are close and see the bullet holes, the patches of splashed blood, the scratches where fingers have dug at the surface of the wall to claw a path to safety. . . And finally the camera comes to a close shot of

Gandhi, matching that of Dyer, whom we have just left. He is surveying the wall in the now empty park numbly, desolately.

Nehru stands a few feet away from him, his mood the same, the same benumbed grief and incredulity.

Resume the wall—Gandhi's point of view. The camera continues its pan—bits of human hair matted in the dried blood, and the bullet-ripped foliage, the well, trampled ground around it, little pieces of clothing. Flies buzz around the debris. Abstractedly, Gandhi touches the bucket rope that lies across the surround. Nehru has moved to the other side of the well. Gandhi lifts his eyes to him . . .

Fade out . . .

Fade in . . .

THE VICE-REGAL PALACE. NEW DELHI. EXTERIOR. DAY.

The imposing capitol building of the British Raj in India. We establish then cut into

GOVERNMENT COUNCIL ROOM. INTERIOR. DAY.

Featuring the Viceroy, Lord Chelmsford.

CHELMSFORD: You must understand, gentlemen, that His Majesty's Government—and the British people—repudiate both the massacre and the philosophy that prompted it.

Chelmsford is pacing along one side of a large conference table. Just in front of this is the "British" side—two generals (a full general and a brigadier), a naval officer, two senior civil servants, a senior police officer. Across from them is the "Indian" side: Gandhi, Nehru, Patel, Jinnah, Azad. This time Gandhi is in the middle and speaks with the full authority of a leader.

The Indian side acknowledges Chelmsford's disclaimer—coolly, but accepting it. That lifts Chelmsford's hopes a little.

CHELMSFORD: What I would like to do is to come to some compromise over the new civil legis—

GANDHI: If you will excuse me, Your Excellency, it is our view that matters have gone beyond "legislation."

It is spoken with the cold determination of a man still angry. It stops Chelmsford in mid-pace.

GANDHI: We think it is time you recognized that you are masters in someone else's home. (*It chills, stiffens; Gandhi proceeds only an iota softer*) Despite the best intentions of the best of you, you must, in the nature of things, humiliate us to control us. General Dyer is but an extreme example of the principle. It is time you left.

The British are stunned almost to speechlessness—the audacity, the impossibility of it—and from Gandhi of all people. The senior civil servant, Kinnoch, is the first to recover.

KINNOCH: With respect, Mr. Gandhi, without British administration, this country would be reduced to chaos.

GANDHI (*patient, ironic*): Mr. Kinnoch, I beg you to accept that there is no people on earth who would not prefer their own bad government to the "good" government of an alien power.

BRIGADIER (*indignantly, choked*): My dear sir—India is British! We're hardly an alien power!

Gandhi and the others just look at him.

Chelmsford is realist enough to recognize that a faux pas has been made, and he strives to get the meeting back on the course he intends.

CHELMSFORD: Even if His Majuesty could waive all other considerations, he has a duty to the millions of his Muslim subjects who are a minority in this realm. And experience has taught that his troops and his administration are essential in order to keep the peace.

He has deliberately if delicately caught the eye of both

Jinnah and Maulana Azad during this. Gandhi knows the trouble this can cause and he answers more for those on his side than the Viceroy's.

GANDHI: All nations contain religious minorities. Like other countries, ours will have its problems. *(Flat, irrevocable)* But they will be ours—not yours.

Its finality is such that for a moment there is no response at all, but then the General smiles.

GENERAL: And how do you propose to make them yours? You don't think we're just going to walk out of India.

His smile flitters cynically on the mouths of the others on his side.

GANDHI: Yes . . . in the end you will walk out. Because one hundred thousand Englishmen simply cannot control three hundred fifty million Indians if the Indians refuse to co-operate. And that is what we intend to achieve—peaceful, non-violent non-co-operation.

He looks at them all, then up at Lord Chelmsford behind them.

GANDHI: Until you yourself see the wisdom of leaving . . . your Excellency.

LATER. THE SAME GOVERNMENT COUNCIL ROOM.

Close shot—a crystal decanter. The top is lifted, whiskey pours.
The camera pulls back. We are still in the Council Room, but time has passed. The Indian delegation has gone, and the British are relaxing as a servant pours.

GENERAL *(mocking his exchange with Gandhi)*: "You don't just expect us to walk out?" "Yes."

And they all laugh.

BRIGADIER: Extraordinary little man! "Nonviolent, non-co-operation"—for a moment I almost thought they were actually going to do something.

There are some smiles, but not all of them are quite so amused.

CHELMSFORD (*thoughtfully*): Yes—but it would be wise to be very cautious for a time. The Anti-Terrorist Act will remain on the statutes, but on no account is Gandhi to be arrested. Whatever mischief he causes, I have no intention of making a martyr of him.

It is an instruction they all find correct.

A FIELD. EXTERIOR. NIGHT.

A roar of approval from a huge crowd. We are featuring two British soldiers, their faces partially lit by a flickering torch light that reveals their tense wariness.

Another angle. And we can see its cause. A huge crowd is gathered around a platform—torches sprinkled through it—and their mood is confident, belligerent. As their defiant roar carries through the night air we see that Gandhi sits cross-legged on the platform. Nehru is with him. Patel, now for the first time in an Indian tunic, and Azad, also in an Indian tunic. Desai, Gandhi's new male secretary, is with them. But it is Ba who is speaking at the microphone, who has brought the shout of defiance from the crowd.

BA (*simple, direct*): . . . but now something worse is happening. When Gandhiji and I were growing up, women wove their own cloth. But now there are millions who have no work because those who can buy all they need from England. I say with Gandhiji, there is no beauty in the finest cloth if it makes hunger and unhappiness.

It is the end of her speech and she makes the *pranam* and turns away. There is applause and noise, but Ba does not acknowledge it; she simply sits cross-legged behind Gandhi, who is talking with Patel and Nehru. At last he rises, and the noise and applause increase to something like chaos.

In close shot we see other British soldiers watching on the perimeter of the crowd and they are now made even more wary by the enthusiasm of this greeting.

Gandhi fiddles with his glasses, preoccupied; finally he

looks out over the crowd and holds up a hand—almost lazily—and gradually, but quite definitely, the crowd stills.

GANDHI: My message tonight is the message I have given to your brothers everywhere. To gain independence we must prove worthy of it.

We intercut with the crowd, listening raptly. Gandhi holds up one finger.

GANDHI: There must be Hindu-Muslim unity—always. (*A second finger.*) Secondly, no Indian must be treated as the English treat us so we must remove untouchability from our lives, and from our hearts.

Neither of these goals is easy, and the audience reaction shows it. Now Gandhi raises the third finger.

GANDHI: Third—we must defy the British.

And the crowd breaks into stamping and applause. Gandhi lets it run for a time, then stills it with the one small gesture as before.

GANDHI: Not with violence that will inflame their will, but with firmness that will open their eyes.

This has sobered the audience somewhat. Now he looks out across them as though seeking something. Then

GANDHI: English factories make the cloth—that makes our poverty. (*A reaction.*) All who wish to make the English see, bring me the cloth from Manchester and Leeds that you wear tonight, and we will light a fire that will be seen in Delhi—and London!

There is an excited stir; he silences it.

GANDHI: And if, like me, you are left with only one piece of homespun—wear it with dignity!

Close shot—the ground. As suitcoats, shirts, vests, trousers, are flung into a pile.
Featuring the two British soldiers—later—on the edge of the crowd, staring off, their faces now brightly lit by darting flames.
Their point of view. A huge triangular pile burns before the

platform, an excited half-naked crowd swirling in the shadows around it.

Resume the two British soldiers. They look at each other with a kind of fear a rampant crowd can excite in those who must hold it. . .

ASHRAM STATION. EXTERIOR. DAY.

The small train station near the ashram. Kallenbach stands by a new (early 1920s) Ford touring car, watching as a train pulls into the station.

As people start to jump off the train he moves forward.

Featuring Patel, getting out of a compartment marked "Second Class." He lugs a bedroll and a bag. Despite the Indian tunic he now wears he cannot help but look and act like the incisive, patrician lawyer he is under the skin. As he moves through the crowded platform

PATEL: Excuse me—just let me get out of your way, please. *(Someone reaches for his bedroll and bag.)* No, thank you, I'll manage.

He looks up; it is Kallenbach who is the insistent "helper."

PATEL *(joyous—it's been a long time)*: Ah, Herman! *(Of the bags)* No, no—don't destroy my good intentions. I'm already feeling guilty about traveling Second Class.

Kallenbach is smilling too. He reaches for the bags again.

KALLENBACH: I do it as a friend—and admirer—not a servant.
PATEL: Ah, in that case!

And grandly, he relinquishes the bags and looks back.

PATEL: Maulana is made of sterner stuff. Our trains met in Bombay, but he's back there in that lot somewhere.

Their point of view. In the chaos of the Third Class we see Maulana Azad coming out of a section of the coach. He is carrying a baby wrapped in rags. The child's mother with two little ones hanging on her has followed him out.

PATEL'S VOICE-OVER: There he is—out Gandhi-ing Gandhi.

Azad hands the woman the baby and she obviously thanks him. He makes a little salaam to her and moves through the confusion of the platform toward the camera.

Resume Patel and Kallenbach.

PATEL (*shaking his head at it all*): When I think what our "beloved Mahatma" asks, I don't know how he ever got such a hold over us. Is he back?

KALLENBACH: Yes. Now that things are moving he's going to write and only take part when it's necessary.

Azad approaches them.

AZAD (*to Patel*): It was a Hindu child and it tried to wet on me.

He and Kallenbach clasp with their free hands, both grinning.

PATEL: Of course. A Muslim beef eater—I'm only surprised he missed.

AZAD: He was a she.

PATAL: Ah, that explains it. (*He grins.*) Well, do I carry your luggage as penance or—

KALLENBACH: There's another passneger—a Miss Slade. (*He turns automatically, as Patel and Azad do, toward the First Class section.*) She's the daughter of an English admiral. (*Patel and Azad look back at him in quick surprise. Kallenbach smiles.*) She's been corresponding with him for a year.

And the camera pans with their glances as they look back with real interest toward the First Class coach.

Porters are unloading the baggage of two or three passengers here and helping some others (English and Indian) to board.

In the foreground we see a tall Indian woman in a red sari. Farther along there is a large stack of luggage being added to by a porter. An English woman is hovering about it. She is well dressed, but rather dreary and unprepossessing, and the camera zooms in toward her.

PATEL: And what does the daughter of an English admiral propose to do in an ashram—sink us?

AZAD (*quietly—his manner*): From the looks of the luggage, yes.

Patel grins. Like most witty men, he loves wit in others.

KALLENBACH: She wants to make her home with us—and Gandhiji has agreed.

Patel groans. They turn back to the train and just as they do, the tall Indian woman in the red sari tips a porter, taking one small bag from him and turns: Mirabehn (Madeleine Slade) is tall, quite pretty and extremely English despite the sari. The minute she turns, she stops on seeing the now startled Kallenbach.

MIRABEHN: You'd be Mr. Kallenbach.

Kallenbach recovers sufficiently to—

KALLENBACH: . . . And you would be Miss Slade.
MIRABEHN (*proudly*): I prefer the name Gandhiji has given me—Mirabehn.

The word means "daughter." Patel and Azad stare at each other in something like bafflement.

THE ROAD TO THE ASHRAM. EXTERIOR. DAY.

An ox labors along in harness. We follow him for a moment, then move along the traces of the harness to the Ford touring car that it is pulling. In the car Kallenbach and Mirabehn sit in the front seat, Patel and Azad in the back.

Closer

KALLENBACH (*of the car*): It was a gift and it only worked a few weeks, but when Gandhi came home he struck on this idea. He calls it his ox-Ford. Comfortable—and yet more our pace.

He does what little steering is necessary and Mirabehn smiles at it all, finding everything delightful. She peers ahead in the direction of the distant ashram.

MIRABEHN: Might Mr. Nehru be there too?
PATEL (*glibly*): The irresponsible young Nehru is in prison—again. Though there is a rumor that under pressure from your country, they will let him out—again.

Mirabehn has turned to look at him. She has the same sophomoric eagerness and intensity as the young Gandhi.

MIRABEHN: You can't know how closely we follow your struggle—

(*to Patel personally*) how many in England admired what you did in Bardoli. It must have taken enormous courage.

PATEL: Well, in this country one must decide if one is more afraid of the government or Gandhi. (*Of Azad, Kallenbach and himself*) For us, it's Gandhi.

Mirabehn is enthralled by the wit, the modesty that underlines the words. She faces Kallenbach.

MIRABEHN (*a note of wonder*): And you're German. . .
KALLENBACH: Yes.
MIRABEHN: And do you feel Indian?

She thinks she does, and that he would want to.

KALLENBACH: No.

It surprises, but it doesn't deflate.

MIRABEHN: But you've been with him so long—why?

Kallenbach, whose size and stillness carry the aura of some great piece of primitive sculpture—solid, true, disturbingly profound—searches inside himself for the answer.

KALLENBACH: . . . I'd come to believe I would never meet a truly honest man. And then I met one.

It is so profoundly simple and deeply felt that it obviously touches the deeply emotional Mirabehn.

GANDHI'S BUNGALOW. EXTERIOR. DAY.

Ba has a spinning wheel on the small porch and Gandhi is sitting next to her with another. He is trying to imitate her action—which is fast and dexterous—and he gets in a terrible jumble. Ba watches, laughing.

BA: Stop—stop . . .

She leans across and tries to extricate his fingers.

BA: God gave you ten thumbs.
GANDHI (*morosely*): Eleven.

And Ba laughs again and Gandhi smiles, tapping her with playful reproval on the top of her bent head. There are footsteps and Gandhi looks up. Patel stands in the doorway. Gandhi's face changes to something like elation. A beat.

GANDHI: Sardar . . .

It means "leader" and it is the name the peasants have
given Patel. Gandhi uses it with an intonation of novelty
and respect. He stands and crosses to Patel, clutching him
emotionally, and it brings a bit of emotion from the sophisticated Patel.
Gandhi holds him back to look at him.

GANDHI: What you've done is a miracle. You have made all India
proud.

Patel gets hold of himself, and affects his usual glib
cynicism.

PATEL: It must have been the only nonviolent campaign ever led
by a man who wanted to kill everybody every day.
GANDHI (*laughs*): Not true! (*He means himself.*) The secret is
mastering the urge.

He smiles again, then, his arm still around Patel's shoulder, he turns to greet the others. Azad looks at him, then
facetiously, as though to put down Patel

AZAD: He came Second Class.

Gandhi laughs again, squeezing Patel's shoulder.

GANDHI: Well, we can't expect miracles all the time. (*Then to
Azad, more soberly*) Your news I understand is not so good.

Azad shakes his head.

AZAD: No.

Gandhi reaches forward and touches his hand, and he sees
Mirabehn on the porch. For a moment their eyes meet and
then Mirabehn moves forward quickly and takes his hand,
kissing it, tears running down her cheek. Gandhi touches
the top of her head.

GANDHI: Come, come—you will be my daughter. . .

LATER. GANDHI'S BUNGALOW.
INTERIOR. TWILIGHT.

The camera is on a row of sandals by the door—Patel's,
Azad's, Desai's, Gandhi's. It pans to the room. Gandhi sit-

ting facing Patel and Azad, Desai in the background, making notes of the discussion. Gandhi is carding fiber to thread as they talk. Mirabehn, seated like the others, is almost in the circle, sitting near Ba, and listening like her. Ba's spinning never stops.

AZAD: . . . but then some rioting broke out between Hindus and Muslims—violent, terrible . . .

Gandhi looks up at Azad, Azad shakes his head solemnly.

AZAD: Whether it was provoked . . . (he shrugs, a hint of suspicion). But it gave them an excuse to impose martial law throughout Bengal. (He looks at Gandhi, shaking his head grimly.) Some of the things the military have done . . .

But he does not go on. It has a terrible sobriety.

GANDHI: Is the campaign weakening?

Azad shakes his head.

AZAD: The marches and protests are bigger if anything but with the censorship here (a nod toward Mirabehn) they know more in England than we do, and it saps the courage to think you may be suffering alone.

Gandhi reaches out and touches his hand.

GANDHI: They are not alone. And martial law only shows how desperate the British are.

He holds Azad's eyes, giving strength. Then he turns to Mirabehn, made more aware of her by Azad's reference. For a moment he looks at her sari.

GANDHI: Is that homespun? Or cotton from Leeds?

The tone suggests he thinks it is homespun. Mirabehn nods, a little choked that his attention is turned to her.

MIRABEHN: I—I sent for it, from here. I dyed it myself.

Gandhi smiles approvingly. Then a shadow—

GANDHI: What do the workers in England make of what we're doing? It must have produced hardship.

Mirabehn beams.

MIRABEHN: It has. But you'd be surprised. They understand—they really do. It's not the workers you have to worry about.

GANDHI: Good. *(A glance toward Ba.)* Ba will have to teach you to spin too.

MIRABEHN: I would rather march.

GANDHI: First spin. Let the others march for a time.

Mirabehn nods and looks resignedly at Ba. Ba is spinning. She smiles.

BA: First lesson: To march, wear shoes, to spin, do not.

Mirabehn looks down at the shoes on her feet—and then at the others and their bare feet—and she looks up in grinning, self-conscious embarrassment. Ba smiles at her affectionately.

BA: I'll teach you all our foolishness, and you must teach me yours.

Mirabehn looks at her, accepting the warmth behind the teasing. It is the beginning of an enduring friendship.

CHAURI CHAURA. EXTERIOR. NIGHT.

A small town. Featuring the faces of six Indian police constables as a torch light parade passes them. There are enough of them in their group to be watching the marchers with a challenging disdain. The marchers are men in loincloths and tunics; they brandish torn and ripped English cloth and shout in unison.

MARCHERS: Home Rule! Long live Gandhi! Buy Indian! Long live Gandhi!

We have cut to the parade—and it is the tail end, going around a corner ahead. Some of the marchers wave their cloth tauntingly at the police. One policeman suddenly steps out and grabs at a piece of cloth waved at him. He pulls it viciously from the marcher.

POLICEMAN: I'll stuff your damn mouth with it!

He chases the marcher and boots him with his foot. Another marcher runs at the policeman, swinging at him with his piece of cloth.

SECOND MARCHER: Leave him alone—he wasn't harming you!

Another angle—sudden. He is whacked across the face with a billy club and falls, clutching his face and spouting blood from his nose.

Another angle. The police are now all attacking, swinging clubs and kicking at the tail-enders of the march. And the tail-enders begin to scream

TAIL-ENDERS: Help! Help us!

as they try to scramble away from the attack. Out of shot we can still hear the disappearing chant: "Home Rule! Long live Gandhi!"

A CONNECTING STREET. EXTERIOR. NIGHT.

The parade is on this street. A tail-ender, blood streaming down his face, runs around the corner.

Close shot—the tail-ender. As he stops

TAIL-ENDER (*screaming*): Help! Help us!

Another angle. Some of the marchers turn at the shout.

RESUME THE POLICE. THE FIRST STREET.

A few of the tail-enders watching, some running clear of the police, some being beaten.

Two police have a man on the ground. One policeman looks up.

POLICEMAN: Hey—

Their point of view. The corner where the parade has disappeared. It is now packed with more marchers, more flooding in from behind.

We see the whole street, the marchers massed near the corner, spread out, staring at the police, who are now frozen in their mayhem, staring off at the marchers.

For a second, utter silence.

And then the police begin to back away from their victims. The marchers start to move forward. The police draw their guns, and the marchers suddenly run at them, a guttural roar, as though they were one single wild beast.

Featuring the police. They start to run, some turning to fire at the pursuing crowd, then running on.

THE POLICE STATION. EXTERIOR. NIGHT.

A small building for this small town. A policeman on duty holds the door and the fleeing police, first one, then two more, then the last three, run into the building.

The crowd surges around it, smashing windows, hurling stones.

Close shot. English cloth shirts pushed together and ignited.

Second close shot. Trousers, already aflame, being hurled through a broken window. All around, the noise of the angry, surging crowd, stones raining on the building. Shouts: "Out—Out!"

Later. A corner of the building engulfed in flames. The camera pulls back and we see the whole building swept with fire. The heat of it keeps the crowd back but they are still shouting "Out—Out!—Out"—and a sudden cheer.

At the door of the flaming building. One policeman appears, his face blackened with soot, his hands up over his head. Another appears in the smoke behind him, and they start to come out—not only the original six but the five or six others who were in the building—rushing suddenly from the heat of the fire.

Close shot—the crowd. We are close on the body of the first policeman as he runs into the crowd and on the instant we see a sword slash at his arm.

Another angle. The crowd massed around the fallen figure, a flash of the sword going up over the heads—a breathless pause—and it comes down again . . . savagely.

Later. The flames of the crumbled building. The crowd has gone and we only hear the roar of the flames. The camera pans across the flames, and we see a skull, charred flesh still clinging to it, the eyes black holes, the teeth bare as it burns in the fire.

JINNAH'S DRAWING ROOM. INTERIOR. DAY.

Close shot—Gandhi. His face drawn, stunned, as he stares emptily at the floor. He is sitting on the carpet in the center of the room. A moment of silence and then we begin to hear the tick of a clock, the sounds of others moving in the room, and finally

PATEL'S VOICE: That's one bit of news they haven't censored.

Another angle. Patel leans with one arm on a table, his mood as devastated as Gandhi's; he is looking at an Indian paper on the table by his hand. A moment then

JINNAH'S VOICE: Oh, it's all over the world. . . . *(ironically)* India's "nonviolence."

He has been standing, looking out of a window. He turns. and tosses a newspaper on a desk. It is the *New York Times* and we just glimpse the picture of the severed head lying in the smoldering ashes.
And now we see Nehru and Azad in the background too. And Desai. Jinnah as usual is in a finely cut European suit, the others are dressed in tunics of homespun as they will be to the end.

NEHRU *(bleakly)*: What can we do?
GANDHI *(sepulchrally)*: We must end the campaign.

They turn to him—a sense of surprise, but they don't really believe he means the statement.

JINNAH: After what they did at the massacre—it's only an eye for an eye.
GANDHI *(he hasn't moved; the same tone)*: An eye for an eye only ends up making the whole world blind. *(Now he looks up at them.)* We must stop.
PATEL *(a baffled smile)*: Gandhiji—do you know the sacrifices people have made?

He looks at him. Gandhi doesn't move. Patel looks up hopelessly at Jinnah. Azad keeps his eyes fixed on Gandhi, sensing, fearing what is going to happen.

JINNAH: We would never get the same commitment again—ever.

He looks at Gandhi with a mounting sense of annoyance. Gandhi is listening, but still withdrawn into himself.

GANDHI: If we obtain our freedom by murder and bloodshed I want no part of it.

NEHRU (*pleading*): It was one incident.

GANDHI (*quietly*): Tell that to the families of the policemen who died.

Jinnah turns away in anger. Patel sighs. Nehru feels help-less but he continues to try.

NEHRU: Bapu—the whole nation is marching. They wouldn't stop, even if we asked them to.

Gandhi stares into nothing—mulling that. Finally

GANDHI: I will ask. And I will fast as penance for my part in arousing such emotions—and I will not stop until they stop.

Nehru stares at him—surprised. Azad is not.

JINNAH (*disgustedly*): God! You can be sure the British won't censor that! They'll put it on every street corner.

Gandhi does not react. And Nehru ignores the thought too, because like Azad his mind is already on the real danger.

NEHRU: But—but Gandhiji people *are* aroused. . . they won't stop.

Gandhi looks up at him—a resigned fatalism.

GANDHI: If I die, perhaps they will . . .

THE ASHRAM. EXTERIOR. TWILIGHT.

Mirabehn walks across the grounds toward Gandhi's bun-galow. She carries a small tray with a pitcher and a glass. We see a few people working in the background, and a mass of people camped near the entrance, some sprawled, some sit-ting, some standing—all waiting.

The steps of Gandhi's bungalow. A doctor in a white tunic sits on the porch, reading. On a small table beside him we see a stethoscope and the equipment to measure blood pressure. He looks up at Mirabehn as she mounts the steps, and nods. Mirabehn reaches the doorway and is suddenly brought up.

GANDHI'S BUNGALOW. THE INTERIOR.
MIRABEHN'S POINT OF VIEW. TWILIGHT.

In the shadows, Ba sits by Gandhi's mat bed. She is holding him as he heaves in a spasm of dry retching, his face to the wall. When he is finished, he lies almost limp in her arms and she gently lowers him to the mat. She strokes his head.

Mirabehn stiffens herself. She is not yet devotee *and* nurse. She removes her sandals and walks across the room.

Ba looks up at her. She glances at the jug and glass, then nods. She turns to Gandhi.

BA (*softly*): I must get ready for evening prayers. Mirabehn is here.

She strokes his sweating head again, touches his shoulder and gets up. For a moment the two women hold each other's gaze, then Ba smiles weakly, and leans her head into the taller Mirabehn's shoulder. With her free hand Mirabehn touches Ba's head. Then Ba straightens, and leaves without looking back.

Mirabehn bends and sits by Gandhi's side.

MIRABEHN: I've brought your drinking water. May I turn you?

Gandhi struggles to turn, and Mirabehn helps him. When he turns we see that his face is wet with sweat from the dry heaving and his hands and arms are quivering and he cannot stop them. She looks at him nervously, then pours a glass from the pitcher.

MIRABEHN: There is little lemon juice in it. That is all.

She turns back, and propping up his head, helps him to sip.

MIRABEHN: Herman has gone to meet Pandit Nehru—there was a telegram. Almost everywhere it has stopped.

Gandhi swallows with difficulty. He pauses, letting his head fall back and she lowers it down to the mat again. He tries to smile.

GANDHI: When it is everywhere, then my prayers will be answered.

Mirabehn looks daunted by his intractability.

GANDHI: Do you find me stubborn?

MIRABEHN *(her own honesty)*: I don't know. . . I know you are right. I don't know that this is right.

Gandhi signals her down to him. She bends so she is looking at the floor and he is speaking almost into her ear.

GANDHI *(hoarse, strained)*: When I despair, I remember that all through history the way of truth and love has always won.

We intercut their faces, very close, as he speaks.

GANDHI: There have been tyrants and murderers, and for a time they can seem invincible. But in the end they always fall. Think of it—always. . . When you are in doubt that that is God's way, the way the world is meant to be . . . think of that.

During the very last of it Mirabehn has turned her face to him, touched with emotion.

GANDHI *(the paternal smile)*: And then—try to do it His way. *(A tear runs down Mirabehn's face. She touches his shoulder. Gandhi just leans his head back in exhaustion.)* And now— could I have another feast of lemon juice?

Mirabehn straightens up, smiling, wiping the tear from her cheek with mock discipline. She starts to pour water from the pitcher into the glass again, then she turns suddenly, her attention caught.

Her point of view. The doorway. Nehru stands in it. Kallenbach and Desai are a step or two behind him.

MIRABEHN: Panditji—come in.

She stands, moving back from Gandhi.

Nehru crosses and kneels in Mirabehn's place. Gandhi looks up at him and his eyes light. He moves his shaking hand out and Nehru clasps it. A moment of personal feeling between them, then

NEHRU: Jinnah, Patel, all of Congress has called for the end of non-co-operation. There's not been one demonstration. All over India people are praying that you will end the fast. They're walking in the streets, offering garlands to the police— and to British soldiers.

It is a victory. Gandhi's face cracks into a tearful grin.

GANDHI (*croaked*): Perhaps—perhaps I have overdone it.

And Nehru chokes with emotion and laughter at the same time. He buries his head on Gandhi's hand, clutching it to him.

THE ASHRAM. EXTERIOR. DAY.

Bright sunshine. A little boy is pulling a goat by a tether. He turns with a bright smile.

LITTLE BOY: Good morning, Bapu!

Reverse angle. Gandhi is walking, holding Ba's shoulder for support with one hand, and Mirabehn's with the other. It is some days later.

GANDHI: Good morning. (*Of the goat*) Don't let her go. If she bumps me I am done for.

The boy grins at Gandhi's feigned alarm.

LITTLE BOY: Don't worry. I milk her every day, she's not—

The sound of a motor disturbs them. Gandhi turns.

His point of view. Coming into the entrance, along the bumpy path are two police cars (early 1920s Morris). They have to stop because they are impeded by Gandhi's ox-Ford.

Four Indian policemen hop quickly out of the second car. A British police superintendent, and his British deputy get more decorously out of the first.

Another angle. Gandhi has turned with his two props, Ba and Mirabehn. The police are approaching him. Kallenbach is running from the fields. Nehru is hurrying from another building carrying sheaves of page proofs. Other ashramites converge from the fields and buildings.

The British police superintendent (who is Scottish) stops before Gandhi.

POLICE SUPERINTENDENT (*a beat*): Sedition.
NEHRU (*it is too absurd*): You can't be serious! This man has just stopped a revolution!

POLICE SUPERINTENDENT (*uncomfortably; he knows*): That's as may be. I only know what I am charged to perform.

Nehru stares at him and the policemen with growing incredulity.

NEHRU: I don't believe it—even the British can't be that stupid!
GANDHI: Panditji—please, help me.

It stops Nehru. He looks at Gandhi and sighs in unmastered frustration, but he moves to Gandhi's side. Gandhi turns to Mirabehn.

GANDHI: You must help Herman—and Ba. (*He releases her, and says more loudly to the others*) I have been on many trips—it is just another trip.

He smiles at them, then slips his free hand on Nehru's shoulder and he turns to the superintendent.

GANDHI: I am at your command.

Featuring Gandhi, Ba and Nehru, as they walk to the car behind the somewhat surprised superintendent.

GANDHI (*to Nehru*): If there is one protest—one riot—a disgrace of any kind, I will fast again.

He looks at Nehru firmly. Nehru knows him well enough now not to argue—even at this, though his face shows the struggle.

GANDHI (*and now he smiles—Gandhi to Nehru, special*): I know India is not ready for my kind of independence. If I am sent to jail, perhaps that is the best protest our country can make at this time. And if it helps India, I have never refused to take His Majesty's hospitality.

He laughs and Nehru struggles to join in the joke.

THE CIRCUIT COURT. AHMEDABAD.
INTERIOR. DAY.

A quiet hum in a packed courtroom. Armed sepoys line the wall.

Featuring Judge Broomfield and the clerk. The Judge is

flipping through documents on the case, a troubled frown on his face. At last, he shuts the folder and nods to the clerk. The clerk turns and says in a moderately loud voice—

CLERK: Call the prisoner to the bar.

The sergeant-at-arms turns and moves to the door at the side of the bench. The courtroom immediately falls silent. The sergeant-at-arms opens the door—a moment—and Gandhi enters slowly. He has recovered a bit more, but he still moves slowly.

Featuring Judge Broomfield. As Gandhi enters, he lowers his glasses, places them on his desk, and rises, facing Gandhi.

Featuring two English court reporters. One nudges the other in astonishment, signaling off toward the judge.

Their point of view. The clerk, confused as well as astonished, sees the judge standing, facing Gandhi in respect, and dutifully, he too stands.

Resume the reporters. A disbelieving exchange of glances, the sound of others standing around them. They glance back.

Full shot—the courtroom. The whole court rises, the astounded reporters the last of all.

Featuring Gandhi. He takes the prisoner's stand. He looks around, a little surprised, a little affected by the demonstration. He looks up at the judge. For a minute their eyes meet, the judge makes a little bow to Gandhi. Gandhi reciprocates . . . and the judge sits down.

Featuring the reporters shrugging incredulously to each other, as they sit once more.

Later. The Advocate General is speaking from a folded journal.

ADVOCATE GENERAL: . . . "Non-co-operation has one aim: the overthrow of the Government. Sedition must become our creed. We must give no quarter, nor can we expect any." (*He looks up at Gandhi.*) Signed M K. Gandhi, in your journal *Young India,* dated twenty-second March of this year. Do you deny writing it?

GANDHI: Not at all. (*To the judge*) And I will save the Court's time, M'Lord, by stating under oath that to this day I believe non-co-operation with evil is a duty. And that British rule of India is evil.

There is a little shock of reaction around the courtroom. The Advocate General smiles with a brittle disdain, then he turns to the judge.

ADVOCATE GENERAL: The Prosecution rests, M'Lord.

The judge nods. He turns, glancing at the empty table for defense counsel, and then to Gandhi.

JUDGE BROOMFIELD: I take it you will conduct your own defense, Mr. Gandhi.

GANDHI: I have no defense, My Lord. I am guilty as charged. (*Then testingly*) And if you truly believe in the system of law you administer in my country, you must inflict on me the severest penalty possible.

It is almost a cruel challenge to the obviously humane Broomfield.

The reporters scribble, watching the Judge even as they write, because the mere doubt in the Judge's face reflects on the whole position of the British to India.

Featuring Judge Broomfield. He lowers his glasses soberly, staring at them for a moment.

JUDGE BROOMFIELD: It is impossible for me to ignore that you are in a different category from any person I have ever tried, or am likely to try.

He looks up at Gandhi and his own respect for him is almost poignantly manifest.

JUDGE BROOMFIELD (*a long beat*): It is nevertheless my duty to sentence you—to six years' imprisonment.

A stunned intake of breath from the whole courtroom, then in absolute silence the clerk scribbles the sentence in his notebook. A pause. The Judge lowers his eyes.

JUDGE BROOMFIELD (*a personal statement, not a real hope*): If however His Majesty's Government could—at some later date—see fit to reduce that term, no one would be better pleased than I.

He folds, and refolds his glasses and then without looking at anyone he rises. The court rises and he walks stiffly to his chambers.

Featuring Gandhi. He stands, staring at Broomfield, and now it is his face that shows the respect.

INDIAN ROAD. EXTERIOR. DAY.

Long shot. From far above the hills we see a car traveling along the road. Its style tells us some years have passed.

Featuring Walker—close. The reporter from the *New York Times*, whom we first saw as a younger man in South Africa. He is in an open car, turning back to look at something, his face intrigued by what he sees.

COLLINS' VOICE-OVER *(English accent)*: Yes, I'm sure that's exactly what they hoped. Put him in prison a few years and with luck he'd be forgotten. And maybe they'd even subdue him . . .

We see from Walker's point of view an Indian woman walking along the road, leading a tall camel that carries sacks of produce. Two young girls in ragged saris walk with her, and a boy of eight leads a smaller camel behind them. They are staring off at the car.

Resume Walker. He swings back around, fascinated with what he is seeing of India. The car is an early 1930s Morris Minor.

COLLINS: Well, he certainly wasn't forgotten! And as soon as he got out he was back tramping the country, preaching non-violence and demanding a free India. Everybody knows another showdown's coming—but when, and over what—

He shrugs, "Nobody knows". . .

WALKER: Well, I read your account of that crowd in Calcutta and that he was twisting the Lion's tail again. . .

Collins has suddenly slowed the car, then swerves around a pair of elephants hauling logs.

WALKER *(falteringly)*: . . . and I knew something had to give. And I was determined to be here when it did.

COLLINS: How does a reporter in Central America learn that Gandhi was born in Porbandar anyway?

WALKER: Oh, I've been a Gandhi buff for a long time.

Collins glances at him in surprise as he steers the car around another procession of camels heading toward the port.

COLLINS: He certainly makes good copy. (*A laugh.*) The other day Winston Churchill called him "that half-naked Indian fakir."

Walker smiles too, but it soon passes.

WALKER: I met him once.

Collins looks at him in real surprise.

COLLINS: You mean Gandhi?

WALKER (*nods*): Back in South Africa . . . (*reflectively*) long time ago.

COLLINS: What was he like?

WALKER: Lots of hair . . . and a little like a college freshman— trying to figure everything out.

COLLINS: Well, he must've found some of the answers . . .

He honks as he goes around a wooden-wheeled cart.

PRANAMI TEMPLE. PROBANDAR. INTERIOR. DAY.

Simple. Austere. Filtered light. Featuring Gandhi—close. He is looking straight ahead.

Reverse angle. Across the emptiness of the temple, Ba faces him.

BA (*a step forward*): "In every worthy wish of yours, I shall be your helpmate."

Another angle featuring Walker and Collins, who are sitting alone, in the cool shadows of the temple, watching with fascination as Gandhi and Ba repeat their marriage ceremony for them, Walker jotting notes occasionally, but his eyes always glued to Gandhi and Ba, who are in part lost in memories and echoes of a significance only they can know.

GANDHI (*a step*): "Take a fourth step, that we may be ever full of joy."

Wide shot. Showing the two of them before the altar of the temple, moving closer to each other.

BA (*a step*): "I will ever live devoted to you, speaking words of love and praying for your happiness."

Close shot—Gandhi.

GANDHI: "Take a fifth step, that we may serve the people."
BA: "I will follow close behind you and help to serve the people."

Featuring Walker, now too entranced by the ceremony, by the depth of layered emotions in Gandhi and Ba's voices and eyes to take any notes. . .

GANDHI: "Take a sixth step, that we may follow our vows in life."
BA: "I will follow you in all our vows and duties."

Ba and Gandhi. Near to meeting now.

GANDHI (*a last step*): "Take the seventh step, that we may ever live as friends."

Ba takes the last step, so that they are face to face. A beat.

BA: "You are my best friend . . . my highest guru, and my sovereign lord."

For a moment their eyes hold—the many dreams, and hopes and pain—the love of many years.
Walker watches, his own face taut with emotion.
Resume Gandhi and Ba. And Gandhi slowly lifts his hand.

GANDHI: Then I put a sweetened wheat cake in her mouth.

He touches Ba's lips with his extended fingers and she kisses them gently.

BA: And I put a sweetened wheat cake in his mouth.

She has lifted her fingers to his mouth and he kisses them gently.
Featuring Walker and Collins both touched, the overtly cynical American obviously even more than the likeable Englishman.
Gandhi turns to them.

GANDHI: And with that we were pronounced man and wife. (*Solemnly*) We were both thirteen. . .

THE BAY. PORBANDAR. EXTERIOR. DAWN.

A tiny, beautiful city rising steeply out of the Arabian Sea with tall, thick-walled buildings, half-fortresses, half-homes, their white walls tinted amber and gold now by the early light of the sun.

Featuring Gandhi, sitting on a promontory watching the sunrise in solemn meditation . . . He becomes aware of the sound of footsteps and he turns to see Walker approaching, a little knapsack over his shoulder. Gandhi smiles. Walker comes to his side, looking out over the bay and city, truly impressed.

WALKER: It's beautiful.
GANDHI: Even as a boy I thought so.

Walker looks down at him. Gandhi scowls up in the early light.

WALKER: Trying to keep track of you is making me change all my sleeping habits.

Gandhi smiles.

GANDHI: And you've come all this way because you think something is going to happen?
WALKER: Hm. (*Then weightedly*) Is it?
GANDHI: Perhaps. I've come here to think about it.

They both watch the waves beat on the shore a moment, the changing hues of the sunrise on the whites of Porbandar.

GANDHI (*musing*): Do you remember much of South Africa?
WALKER: A great deal.
GANDHI: I've traveled so far—and thought so much. (*He smiles in self-mockery, and turns toward the city.*) As you can see, my city was a sea city—always filled with Hindus and Muslims and Sikhs and Jews and Persians. (*He looks at Walker.*) The temple where you were yesterday is of my family's sect, the Pranami. It was Hindu of course but the priests used to read from the Muslim Koran and the Hindu Gita, moving from one to the other as though it mattered not at all which book was read as long as God was worshipped.

He looks out to sea, and we intercut his face with Walker's, the sea, and the town itself as the sun turns it white.

GANDHI: When I was a boy I used to sing a song in that temple: "A true disciple knows another's woes as his own. He bows to all and despises none. . . Earthly possessions hold him not." Like all boys I said the words, not thinking of what they meant or how they might be influencing me. (*He looks at Walker . . . then out to the sea again, shaking his head.*) I've traveled so far . . . and all I've done is come back home.

Walker studies him as this profound man reaches, in his middle years, a profound insight.

Featuring Gandhi staring out to sea, his mind locked in reflection, and suddenly his head lifts, his eyes become alert, he is caught by some excitement which he weighs for a moment, then he stands, his manner suddenly tingling with optimism.

Walker stares at him, then at what Gandhi seems to be looking at.

His point of view. The waves lapping the shore below them.

Walker turns back to Gandhi, puzzled. But there is no mistaking the sudden glow in Gandhi's face.

WALKER: You know what you're going to do.

Gandhi looks at him, a teasing smile.

GANDHI: It would have been very uncivil of me to let you make such a long trip for nothing.

The grin broadens, and then he starts briskly down the promontory. Walker scrambles up after him.

WALKER: Where are you going?

Gulls fly over them, squawking in the growing light. Gandhi pauses, looking up at the gulls, then back down to the sea.

GANDHI: I'm going back to the ashram (*then firmly*) and then I'm going to prove to the new Viceroy that the King's writ no longer runs in India!

He turns from the sea to Walker, his eyes confident,

elated, then he continues on down the promontory. Still baffled, Walker glances at the sea, at him, then hurries after. Full shot. The waves running against the shore . . .

LORD IRWIN'S OFFICE. INTERIOR. DAY.

Close shot—the Viceroy, a "new one," Lord Irwin.

IRWIN: Salt?

Another angle. He is looking in astonishment at his principal secretary. His ADC, a general, a brigadier, a senior police officer are with him. Like him they hold the same offices, but are a new team.

PRINCIPAL SECRETARY: Yes, sir. He is going to march to the sea and make salt.

Irwin looks at him, still trying to penetrate the significance of the act. The senior police officer helps.

SENIOR POLICE OFFICER: There is a Royal Monopoly on the manufacture of salt, sir. It's illegal to make it or sell it without a Government license.

Irwin has listened; it's beginning to make a little sense.

IRWIN: All right—he's breaking the law. What will he be depriving us of, two rupees of salt tax?

PRINCIPAL SECRETARY: It's not a serious attack on the revenue, sir. Its primary importance is symbolic.

IRWIN: Don't patronize me, Charles.

The principal secretary blanches.

PRINCIPAL SECRETARY: No, sir. I—in this climate, sir, nothing lives without water—or salt. Our absolute control of it is a control on the pulse of India.

Irwin looks at his ADC, then paces a bit, pondering it.

IRWIN: And that's the basis of this "Declaration of Independence"?

SENIOR POLICE OFFICER: Yes, sir. The day he sets off everyone is supposed to raise the flag of "Free India." Then he walks some two hundred and forty miles to the sea and makes salt.

A moment as Irwin considers it, then it is the general who speaks.

GENERAL: I say ignore it. Let them raise their damn flags, let him make his salt. It's only symbolic if we choose to make it so.

PRINCIPAL SECRETARY (*pointedly*): He's going to arrive at the sea on the anniversary of the massacre at Amritsar.

Irwin has turned to him. And this makes up his mind.

IRWIN: General Edgar is right—ignore it. Mr. Gandhi will find it's going to take a great deal more than a pinch of salt to bring down the British Empire.

He is concerned enough to be angry, but certain enough to be dogmatic.

THE ASHRAM. EXTERIOR. DAWN.

It is very early, the light just beginning to break, and we are looking out across the river toward the distant town, and against the pink glow of the sky we can see people in groups wading across the river toward the ashram. And suddenly a mass of people, hidden by the embankment, appear at the top of the steps coming up from the river, and the camera lifts slightly with their movement and we see that they are but the forerunners of a long tendril of humanity that stretches across the river, all the way back to the distant outskirts of the city.

And around the ashram many fires are burning, people are cooking breakfast, some are packing knapsacks for the journey, others are strewing the path from the ashram with leaves.

GANDHI'S BUNGALOW. INTERIOR. DAWN.

Quiet, just the buzz of activity from outside the building. Gandhi lies on a mat and Ba and Mirabehn are massaging him with oil as he checks page proofs, an oil lamp by his side. Nehru sits cross-legged next to him, taking the proofs as Gandhi finishes them. Maulana Azad sits to one side. Behind them Desai is making notes on Gandhi's instructions.

GANDHI (to Nehru): . . . the real test will come if I am arrested. If there is violence we lose all our moral advantage. This time it mustn't happen.

He looks at Nehru and Azad solemnly to emphasize the point. Nehru nods; a little smile.

NEHRU: We're not beginners anymore. We've been trained by a strict sergeant major.

He means Gandhi of course, and Gandhi accepts the reference, but it is the acceptance of the strict sergeant major: "Don't fail me." Then he looks to Azad.

GANDHI: If I'm taken, Maulana is to lead the march. If he is arrested, Patel, then Kripalani, then yourself.

Nehru nods. Ba moves to massage the top of Gandhi's head.

BA: You should be relaxing.

Gandhi grins, looking at Mirabehn, who is massaging his legs.

GANDHI: I'm sure I'm fit for at least five hundred miles.
MIRABEHN: You should ride the pony. It is not necessary to walk to prove the point.

Gandhi looks at Nehru, a benign shrug.

GANDHI: I have two of them bossing me now.

Nehru smiles. He stands, having taken the last proof sheet. Azad rises with him.

NEHRU: We must get these to the printer. (He looks down at Gandhi.) I know it will succeed. Even my mother is prepared to march.

Gandhi is pleasurably impressed with that.

GANDHI: And Jinnah?
NEHRU (a beat): He's waiting. He's not prepared to accept it will mean as much as you think.
GANDHI (smiles confidently): Wait and see . . . wait and see. . .

He leans back and closes his eyes. Ba rubs his head soothingly. Nehru bends and squeezes his arm in farewell. Gandhi nods, not opening his eyes. Nehru and Azad smile at Ba and leave.

THE ASHRAM. LATER. EXTERIOR. DAY.

The sun higher, but still early light. A green, white and saffron flag (the colors of India) is pulled up an uneven pole. The sound of gentle clapping.

Gandhi is off to one side, just in front of the veranda of his bungalow, not paying attention to the ceremony. Ba and Mirabehn watch from the veranda as Pyarelal (Desai's new assistant), with a knapsack over his own shoulders, hands Gandhi his. As Gandhi slips it on, the ashramite boy whom we saw with the goat hands him a long staff. And Gandhi moves around the edge of the bungalow, heading toward the entrance of the ashram.

A long line of ashramites and marchers stretches from opposite the flagpole to the entrance of the ashram. As Gandhi walks briskly along it, they turn, ready to follow him.

When he nears the entrance Gandhi sees Walker standing in front of a collection of newsmen, cameramen, a newsreel crew. He begins to smile, Walker returns it. Gandhi pauses by him.

GANDHI (of the press): You've done me a great service.
WALKER (a grin, then a play on Gandhi's words to him): It would have been uncivil of me to have let you make such a long trip for nothing.

Gandhi smiles. He turns back toward his bungalow. Ba and Mirabehn stand there watching, Desai with them. Gandhi holds their gaze a second, then turns and starts forward. Pyarelal takes up a position next to him, the marchers follow.

Featuring Walker. He steps back, letting Gandhi proceed into the range of the cameras on his own. The crowd around the entrance throws flowers in Gandhi's path, some calling out, "Long live Mahatma Gandhi!"

Gandhi passes the cameramen and starts along the trail.

THE PATH TO GANDHI'S ASHRAM. EXTERIOR. DAY.

A thinner crowd here, but going all along the path. To one side we see two police cars drawn up, and several policemen (a British officer, a British sergeant, and four Indian constables) lined up near them.

As Gandhi nears them Walker moves up beside him. Some of the newspaper cameramen trot behind to get the picture of Gandhi's arrest. Among the newsmen we see Collins.

Featuring Gandhi and Walker, Pyarelal just behind them all glancing ahead at the police, who are now quite near.

WALKER: Is it over if they arrest you now?
GANDHI: Not if they arrest me—or a thousand—or ten thousand. (*He looks at Walker.*) It is not only generals who know how to plan campaigns.

Walker smiles—a little uneasily—for they are now near the police. Gandhi nods to them amiably as he passes along in front of them. Walker is turning, watching for a move from the police but begins to grasp that there may be none. He hurries along closer to Gandhi again, one eye still on the police.

WALKER: What if they don't arrest you? What if they don't react at all?

Gandhi glances at him. Walker too wears a knapsack. Gandhi nods to it, though never breaking his pace.

GANDHI: Do you still have your notebook? (*Walker fumbles for it; Gandhi goes right on talking.*) The function of a civil resister is to provoke response. And we will continue to provoke until they respond, or they change the law. They are not in control—we are. That is the strength of civil resistance.

He nods politely toward the British police officer at the end of the police line. Walker stops, letting the procession march on by him, looking at the British police officer, then writing busily in his notebook. Collins stops by him.

COLLINS: What'd he say?
WALKER (*wryly*): He said he's in charge . . .

AN INDIAN VILLAGE. EXTERIOR. DAY.

A dusty approach to a dusty little village. Both sides of the track are lined with peasants holding flower petals and leaves, all gazing expectantly down the road. Behind them the village is strung with the green, white and saffron colors of Independence.

Two large policemen stand arms-akimbo at the front of them all, their postures imposing and threatening, though the impression is somewhat weakened by the children skirting around them.

A little band of drummers and flute players suddenly begins to play. The crowd starts to jump up to see, and the flower petals begin to float in the sky. "Gandhi! Long live Mahatma Gandhi!"

Another angle. Gandhi and the procession of marchers and ashramites stride down the dusty road toward them.

A newsreel truck and crew ride along about two-thirds of the way back. A car of cameramen and reporters tails at the end.

Featuring Gandhi. He looks at Walker, walking along a few paces behind him, at the side of the procession. He is wiping sweat from his face.

GANDHI: Are you going to walk all the way?

WALKER (a weary grin): My name is Walk-er. And I intend to report it the way it is.

Gandhi smiles and turns back. He shakes his head.

GANDHI (to himself): "My name is Walk-er" . . .

And grinning at it, he passes by the policemen and into the cheers of the crowd.

Long shot, high. As the procession trails into the village, we see several villagers, knapsacks or bundles strung over their shoulders, run around the police and join the end of the procession.

A FIELD BY THE ROAD. EXTERIOR. NIGHT.

In the dark a large group of students comes stumbling, laughing, across the ditch that separates the road from the field. The student leader gets clear of the ditch and comes upon Pyarelal and Walker. They are standing near a group of American newsmen playing poker by a campfire. He addresses Pyarelel good-naturedly.

STUDENT LEADER: We've come to join the march. What do we do?

PYARELEL (*bluntly*): Be sure you're awake in the morning. (*It comes from a knowledge of students. He smiles and nods off.*) Find a place to sleep.

The student leader follows his gaze and the camera pans off with his glance. We see that the numbers have grown immensely. Fires dot the field and spread and spread and spread. Behind Walker and Pyarelal the newsreel truck and three cars for reporters are spread out around the fires. We identify a couple of Frenchmen and a Japanese. Walker looks at Pyarelel and shakes his head in wonder at it all.

TREE. EXTERIOR. DAWN.

A small Indian boy is high in a dead tree. Below him a couple of bone-thin cattle graze in the early light as he stares off.

DUSTY ROAD. BOY'S POINT OF VIEW.
EXTERIOR. DAWN.

The huge procession stretched out along the road.
Resume the boy. He grins as though he is privy to some great secret.

A "Y" JUNCTION OF TWO COUNTRY ROADS.
EXTERIOR. DAY.

A blunt, rotund, powerful-looking woman (Sarojini Naidu) in an outrageously colorful sari strides along the dusty road as though she could cover another thousand miles—and means to. The sound of hundreds of marching feet, of cars, some distant singing. The camera lifts and pulls back. We see that Naidu is marching just behind Gandhi, like a determined lieutentant, and that the procession has grown even greater. Two newsreel trucks now, four cars of reporters, some people riding donkeys, some walking with camels trailing, loaded with belongings.

And at the "Y" junction the newsreel crews suddenly go into action because another enormous procession is waiting to join the first, mingling already, making one immense column of humanity.

And as they pass the camera up close we see an extraordinary variety of participants: old, young, students, peasants, ladies in saris and jewels, Muslims, Hindus, Sikhs, Christian nuns, Untouchables, merchants, some vigorous and determined, others disheveled, tired and determined.

Suddenly the sound of waves and gentle wind.

THE BEACH AT DANDI. EXTERIOR. DAY.

The camera closing fast (helicopter) as the silhouette of a man appears running up a sand dune, lifting his arms to the sky and the camera sweeps over him and up, revealing a crescent of beach and ocean, and for a second it holds on the sea as it did at Porbandar, then pivots to the truly astronomical crowd thronging the shore, an immense wheel of human beings, and in its hub a gathering around Gandhi. We descend on that center, recognizing the newsmen, Walker, Pyarelal, Sarojini Naidu, and at last Gandhi picking up a handful of natural salt and lifting it high.

During the last of this

GANDHI'S VOICE-OVER: Man needs salt as he needs air and water. This salt comes from the Indian Ocean. (*The salt crystals are added to an urn already partially full. The camera pulls back and Gandhi lifts the urn. All around him the pressing crowd: newsreel cameramen, reporters—Walker, Collins, Naidu, Pyarelal. Firmly*) Let every Indian claim it as his right!!

A wide-angle shot.

Gandhi in the center of the wildly cheering crowd, the camera pulling back and back . . . and the shot becomes black and white, and we hear the music of Movietone News.

ANNOUNCER'S VOICE-OVER: . . . and so once more the man of nonviolence has challenged the might of the British Empire.

And with that we get the Movietone Music tag and as the film fades, the lights go up on

LORD IRWIN'S OFFICE. INTERIOR. DAY.

A couple of civil servants move about to raise the window shades while Lord Irwin stares at the blank screen set up in his office. The general, the brigadier, the senior police officer, Irwin's ADC and the principal secretary are all present. The two men who ran the projector are quietly dismantling it.

Finally, Irwin turns to the senior police officer, who fidgets, but answers the implied questions.

SENIOR POLICE OFFICER: They're making it everywhere, sir—mobs of them—publicly. Congress leaders are selling it on the streets of Delhi.

Irwin sighs.

BRIGADIER: We're being made fools of around the world!
GENERAL: Isn't there any instruction from London?

Irwin nods.

IRWIN: We're required to stop it. *(He stands, his mind made up.)* And stop it we will. *(He looks at the senior police officer.)* I don't care if we fill the jails, stop it. Arrest anyone, any rank—except Gandhi. We'll cut his strength from under him. And then we'll deal with the Mahatma.

For the first time he is truly angry.

A WALL BY A BEACH. EXTERIOR. DAY.

A young British subaltern trots up to the wall and looks down. His face falls.

BRITISH SUBALTERN: Oh, my God!

The beach. Subaltern's point of view. Packed with people making salt, selling salt, buying salt.

Resume the British subaltern. He looks back.

His point of view. Behind him there is an open military truck and about twenty sepoys. Formidable for an ordinary crowd, nothing to handle this. The subaltern stiffens bravely and signals the men somewhat unconvincingly from the truck.

SUBALTERN: Right—jump to it—clear this beach!

SMALL WAREHOUSE. INTERIOR. DAY.

Men, women and children are making little paper packets of salt from piles heaped along long tables. A group of policemen barge into the room, knocking tables and salt and paper in every direction with their lathis, seizing some of the volunteers for arrest.

In the chaos an old man calmly picks up a piece of paper from the floor, a handful of salt, and folds another packet.

A WIDE CITY STREET. EXTERIOR. DAY.

Nehru is on the back of a big open truck that is stationary in the street. The truck is loaded with boxes that contain salt packets and Nehru and eight or nine others are selling them to people who flock about the truck. The sound of horses. Nehru lifts his head.

Mounted Indian police are coming down either side of the street, a wave of foot police running forward down the center.

Some of the people run, others deliberately stand fast.

The mounted police converge on the truck. Nehru is grabbed, and hurled so that he half falls, half leaps to the street. One of the men with him is knocked along the ground by a policeman. He is young and vigorous and he swivels on the ground as though to strike back. Nehru lunges toward him.

NEHRU: No violence, Zia!

And a lathi is brought smashing across the side of Nehru's head. He is knocked to his knees; blood streams from his head. He feels the side of his head, the blood soaking his hand. He struggles to his feet, facing the policeman who has struck him.

NEHRU (repeating quietly, as though to Zia): . . . no violence.

It stops the policeman for a second, and a sergeant suddenly intrudes, recognizing Nehru.

SERGEANT: You're Nehru—
NEHRU: I'm an illegal trader in salt.

The sergeant sighs grimly.

LORD IRWIN'S OFFICE. INTERIOR. NIGHT.

The desk lights are on. Irwin, the senior police officer, the principal secretary. Tension, fatigue, frustration as the senior police officer outlines the situation.

SENIOR POLICE OFFICER: . . . There's been no time to keep figures, but there must be ninety—a hundred thousand under arrest. *(Grimly, incredibly)* And it still goes on.
IRWIN *(impatiently)*: Who's leading them?
SENIOR POLICE OFFICER: I don't know! Nehru, Patel, almost every Congress Official is in jail . . . and their wives and their children—we've even arrested Nehru's mother.
PRINCIPAL SECRETARY *(shrewdly)*: Has there been any violence?
SENIOR POLICE OFFICER *(distracted, offhand)*: Oh, in Karachi the police fired on a crowd and killed a couple of people and— *(and this hurts)* and in Peshawar the Deputy Police Commissioner lost his head and . . . and opened fire with a machine gun. *(He looks up at them quickly, defensively.)* But he's facing a disciplinary court! You can't expect things like that not to happen when—
IRWIN *(dryly)*: I believe the question was intended to discover if there was any violence on their side.

The senior police officer looks up, realizing his gaffe and wishes desperately he could relive the last couple of minutes.

SENIOR POLICE OFFICER: Oh, no, sir—no, I'm afraid not.
PRINCIPAL SECRETARY *(again the Machiavellian mind)*: Perhaps if we arrested Gandhi, it might—

He means incite violence. The Viceroy ponders it—favorably.

IRWIN *(to senior police officer)*: He's addressed this letter directly to you, has he?

SENIOR POLICE OFFICER: Yes, sir, he has. The usual—India's salt belongs to India—but then he says flatly that he personally is going to lead a raid tomorrow on the Dharasana Salt Works.

IRWIN (*calmly*): Thank him for his letter, and put him in jail.

The senior police officer is brought up by the chill directness of it. He looks at Irwin and the principal secretary for a moment in uncertainty. Then

SENIOR POLICE OFFICER: Yes, sir. Yes, sir. It will be my pleasure.

As he turns to leave Irwin speaks—almost offhandedly.

IRWIN: And Fields, keep that salt works open.

The senior police officer stares at him, then

SENIOR POLICE OFFICER: (*delighted*): Yes, sir!

DHARASANA SALT WORKS. EXTERIOR. DAY.

Barbed wire stretches on either side of the stockade-like entrance. Above the gate we see the sign DHARASANA SALT WORKS. Before it six British police officers and two Indian police officers command a large troop of Indian policemen. They face their opposition, unmoving, tense. The camera pans from them, across a sloping dip in the ground, to a huge group of volunteers lining up to face the police as tautly as the police face them.

Walker is off to one side, climbing to stand in the back of Collins' car. He watches, looking tensely from one group to the other, almost terrified by what seems about to happen.

Collins leans against the back of the car near him, watching with an equally appalled expectancy. There are two other reporters near them.

From Walker's point of view. We see Mirabehn and some Indian women quietly placing stretchers and tables of bandages near a group of tents where the volunteers have been housed.

Walker turns back to the two opposing groups at the Salt Works entrance. We hear only a shuffle of feet, the clank of a lathi against a metal police buckle. The air itself seems breathless with tension.

Featuring Azad. He has approached the chief police officer. He stops before him politely.

AZAD: I would like admission to the Works.
CHIEF POLICE OFFICER (*equally politely*): I am sorry, sir. That cannot be allowed.

Azad looks at him a second, then glances at the troops. He is clearly afraid, but there is an air of tragic inevitability in his face.
He moves back to address the volunteers.

AZAD: Last night they took Gandhiji from us. They expect us to lose heart or to fight back. We will not lose heart, we will not fight back. In his name we will be beaten. As he has taught us, we will not raise a hand. "Long live Mahatma Gandhi!"

He turns and starts down the dip toward the gate and the waiting lathis of the police.
A series of shots, as Azad leads the first row of volunteers down and up the dip.
We intercut Walker, frozen, watching the inevitable onslaught, the British police commanding officer ready to give the first order.

POLICE COMMANDING OFFICER (*finally*): Now!

And with the volunteers a foot from them, the police strike with their lathis. A groan of empathic anguish from the waiting volunteers, but then we get
A series of shots.
As the next row moves forward and the horror of the one-sided mayhem proceeds heads are cracked, faces split, ribs smashed, and yet one row of volunteers follows another, and another into the unrelenting police, who knock bleeding bodies out of the way, down into the dip, swing till sweat pours from their faces and bodies.
And through it we intercut with Mirabehn and the Indian women rescuing the wounded, carrying them on stretchers to be bandaged. We see Walker helping once or twice, turning, watching, torn between being a professional spectator and a normal human being. And always the volunteers coming, never stopping, never offering resistance.
And finally on sound there is an insistent click, click, click, like a thud of the lathis but becoming clearly the slap of an impatient hand on a telephone cradle and out of the carnage of the salt works we dissolve to

A SMALL INDIAN STORE. INTERIOR. TWILIGHT.

Close shot—a telephone cradle being pounded.

Walker is at the phone at a table in the corner of the small, cluttered store. His clothes are matted with blood and dirt.

WALKER (*into the phone*): Hello! Ed! Ed! Goddammit, don't cut me off! (*Then suddenly he's through.*) Ed! Okay—yeah—right.

And he continues urgently reading the story that lies on his notes on the little stand before him.

WALKER: "They walked, with heads up, without music, or cheering, or any hope of escape from injury or death." (*His voice is taut, harshly professional.*) "It went on and on and on. Women carried the wounded bodies from the ditch until they dropped from exhaustion. But still it went on."

He shifts the mangled notes and comes to his last paragraph. He speaks it trying only half successfully to keep the emotion from his voice.

WALKER: "Whatever moral ascendance the West held was lost today. India is free for she has taken all that steel and cruelty can give, and she has neither cringed nor retreated." (*On Walker close. His sweating, blood and dirt-stained face near tears.*) "In the words of his followers, 'Long live Mahatma Gandhi.' "

LORD IRWIN'S OFFICE. INTERIOR. DAY.

Silence. The camera moves across the empty room and discovers Irwin, standing by himself, looking out of the window down into the street.

Closer. His numb, motionless face is stirred to consciousness by something outside. He focuses somberly on it.

RAJPATH AND VICE-REGAL PALACE. IRWIN'S POINT OF VIEW. EXTERIOR. DAY.

Through the formal entrance comes a single black car. A motorcycle policeman precedes it.

VICE-REGAL PALACE. EXTERIOR. DAY.

The black car pulls up before the front of the palace and stops. There is no sign of activity. It is as though the building and grounds are deserted except for Irwin alone in his office.

Gandhi gets out of the car. He too is alone. In his dhoti and shawl he starts to mount the grand stairs.

Wide angle. The great palace, the magnificent entrance, and the little man in the dhoti, who in a sense has conquered it all, marching to the great doors. Two Gurkhas spring to attention and the doors are swung open.

LORD IRWIN'S OFFICE. INTERIOR. DAY.

The principal secretary, with a look of faint distaste for someone out of shot, discreetly moves out of the doors, and closes them behind him.

Featuring Gandhi, just inside the door. He is looking across the wide office.

GANDHI: I am aware that I must have given you much cause for irritation, your Excellency. I hope it will not stand between us as men.

Reverse angle. Irwin in shadows behind his desk looking, still, in some kind of shock, staring at Gandhi.

IRWIN: Mr. Gandhi, I have instructions to request your attendance at an All-Government Conference in London to discuss—to discuss the possible Independence of India.

He faces Gandhi stiffly.

The whirr of a camera, and a swift cut to

A SUCCESSION OF BLACK-AND-WHITE "NEWSREEL" SEQUENCES OF GANDHI'S VISIT TO ENGLAND AND THE ALL-GOVERNMENT CONFERENCE.

Wide screen, but slightly under-cranked with the bad cutting and predictable music of the old newsreels.

A. Gandhi, Mirabehn and Gandhi's secretary, Desai, waving goodbye from the boat deck of their ship as it sails—

Mirabehn is holding the tether of a goat—all of them smiling at the camera like voyagers everywhere.

B. Gandhi on the steps of Kingsley Hall in the East End of London being greeted by a cheering crowd. Mirabehn holds an umbrella over him as he takes a bouquet from a little child. The now gray-haired Charlie Andrews beams possessively at his side.

C. Gandhi, in his dhoti, waving to a small crowd as he enters the gates of Buckingham Palace. A London bobby watches.

D. Gandhi, taking his seat at the conference table among the formally—in some Maharajahs' cases, elaborately—dressed delegates. A gavel is struck and Ramsay MacDonald begins his opening address.

MACDONALD: I think our first duty is to recognize that there is not one India, but several: a Hindu India, a Muslim India, an India of Princely States. And all these must be respected—and cared for—not just one.

Beneath its unctuous political veneer it is blatantly divisive and clearly reveals the true intent of the Conference. As Gandhi looks at MacDonald, we read on his face his perception of the sad truth.

E. Gandhi, Mirabehn and Charlie walking under an umbrella in the rain, their heads bent in glum conversation.

F. Gandhi being welcomed and kissed by a group of mill-workers outside a large mill entrance identified by the sign GREENFIELD COTTON MILL, LANCASHIRE. He is hugged and squeezed by some hefty female millworkers, all grinning happily, Gandhi not least.

G. Gandhi in a radio studio, seated at a table, a large microphone labeled "CBS" before him, technicians and Mirabehn in the glass booth behind him, Walker across the table from him, the "On the Air" sign bright . . .

GANDHI (to Walker): Do I speak into that?

Walker cringes, glancing at the lighted "On the Air" sign. He signals "Yes" frantically.

GANDHI: Are they ready? Do I start?

He glances at the booth. Everybody including Walker

and Mirabehn are nodding "Yes." Gandhi shrugs, grins at everyone's excitement, and begins.

GANDHI: I am glad to speak to America where so many friends exist that I know only in my heart.

As the speech continues in the thin, static-y tones of thirties' radio, we see Mirabehn and the technicians listening in the control room./Walker, across the table from Gandhi./ The outside of Broadcasting House./ The Empire State Building and Manhattan./ A mid-western farmhouse./ A thirties' radio set in a thirties' American living room./ A family, listening, kids playing on the floor, half ignoring it, the mother ironing, the father in an armchair, a newspaper open.

GANDHI'S VOICE (continuing over all): I think your interest and the world's has fallen on India, not only because we are struggling for freedom, but because the way we are doing so is unique as far as history shows us. Here in Europe mighty nations are, it seems, already contemplating another war, though I think they, and all the world, are sick to death of bloodspilling. All of us are seeking a way out, and I flatter myself that perhaps the ancient land of India will offer such a way. If we are to make progress we must not repeat history, but make history. And I myself will die before I betray our belief that love is a stronger weapon than hate.

H. Gandhi shaking hands with MacDonald outside No. 10 Downing Street, MacDonald smiling the politician's smile, Gandhi smiling rather sadly.
I. Gandhi on the deck of a boat, sitting on a deck chair, wrapped in blankets, staring somberly out to sea. Reverse angle: the wake of the boat in the vast ocean.

THE ASHRAM. EXTERIOR. DAY.

The gentle sounds of the country. A girl of twelve leads a limping goat slowly across the grass. She pauses and looks up questioningly.
Reverse angle—close. Gandhi is watching from the porch of his bungalow. We can tell he is sitting and turned to

watch the goat, but we see only him and a portion of the bungalow behind him.

GANDHI: It is only a sprain. Take her to the river, and we'll make a mud-pack for her. Go—I won't be long.

He turns back.

Another angle. He is spinning (expertly), and gathered on the porch with him are Nehru and Jinnah and Patel and Azad and Kripalani. Desai and Pyarelal are inconspicuously in attendance as always, Pyarelal now clearly sharing Desai's role as secretary.

JINNAH: So the truth is, after all your travels, all your efforts, they've stopped the campaign and sent you home empty-handed.

He is in his white suit, the black-ribboned pince-nez. He sits on a wicker chair, Nehru and Patel lean against the railing, Azad and Kripalani sit on the floor like Gandhi.

GANDHI: They are only clinging to old dreams (*looks up from his spinning to Jinnah*) and trying to split us in the old way. But the will has gone—Independence will drop like a ripe apple. The only question is when (*another glance at Jinnah*) and how.

NEHRU: I say when is now—and we will determine how.

JINNAH: Precisely.

Gandhi winds up what he has done, and starts to rise.

GANDHI: They are preparing for war. I will not support it, but I do not intend to take advantage of their danger.

PATEL (*blithely, but to the point*): That's *when* you take advantage.

Gandhi has moved toward the steps. He stops and looks at Patel. A wry, gentle smile.

GANDHI: No. That is just another way of striking back. We have come a long way together with the British. When they leave we want to see them off as friends. (*He starts down the steps and heads for the river.*) And now, if you'll excuse me, there is something I must attend to.

Featuring Nehru. He looks at Jinnah and shrugs. Jinnah

takes it less philosophically and his eyes burn with anger as he watches Gandhi head for the young girl with the injured goat.

NEHRU (*resignedly*): "Mud packs."

TRAIN STATION. INTERIOR. DUSK.

Gandhi is moving with the stream of passengers disembarking from the Third Class section. Ba and Mirabehn are struggling along behind him, Desai and Pyarelal completing the little group. They pass a newspaper stand: "Hitler's Armies Sweep On." As they move out into the flux of the station we see many uniforms, the sense of a nation readying for war.

A British captain stands before a full platoon of Indian troops.

As Gandhi approaches, a British Lt. Colonel and his Adjutant (a Captain) move out from one side of the troops.

BRITISH COLONEL: Mr. Gandhi—sir.

Gandhi stops, looks up at him, at the troops behind him.

BRITISH COLONEL: I have instructions to inquire as to the subject of your speech tonight.

Gandhi shakes his head with a weary grin.

GANDHI: The value of goat's milk in daily diet. (*Into his eyes*) But you can be sure I will also speak against war.

The British Colonel signals back to the troops.

BRITISH COLONEL: I'm sorry, sir. That can't be allowed.

As a detail marches up to them, the colonel's adjutant speaks gently to Ba.

ADJUTANT: It's all right, Mrs. Gandhi. I have orders to return with you and your companion to the Mahatma's ashram.

BA: If you take my husband, I intend to speak in his place.

She stares at the adjutant belligerently. He looks flummoxed.

Later. Long shot—high. The colonel and his adjutant striding toward the exit of the station. Following behind them, a detail of six soldiers accompanying Gandhi. The camera tracks across the platform and we see they are being followed by a detail of six soldiers accompanying Ba. And the camera tracks again and we see they are being followed by a detail of six soldiers accompanying Mirabehn!

A WINDING BUMPY ROAD. EXTERIOR. DAY.

A jeep bounces along the road. It is driven by an American lieutenant and his passenger is a woman dressed in an American War Correspondent's uniform (Margaret Bourke-White). As the jeep passes the camera we pan with it and see the walls of a palace ahead.

BOURKE-WHITE: Stop! Wait a minute!

The jeep slithers to a stop, and Bourke-White grabs a camera that is strapped around her, stands, and takes a picture of the palace.

AGA KHAN'S PALACE. BOURKE-WHITE'S POINT OF VIEW. EXTERIOR. DAY.

The palace looks evocative—a lonely, incongruous building.

A WINDING BUMPY ROAD. EXTERIOR. DAY.

LIEUTENANT: It was the Aga Khan's palace, but they've turned it into a prison.

Bourke-White slips back down into her seat; we see the arm band on her jacket: "Press." The lieutenant starts the jeep up and they head toward the gate, where we see a British soldier on guard.

LIEUTENANT (shouting over the motor): They've got most of the leading Congress politicians in this one. But Nehru and some others are over in Dehra Dun. Your timing's pretty lucky. They had your Mr. Gandhi cut off from the press but last month his personal secretary died and they've let up on the restrictions.

Bourke-White just absorbs it, staring at the palace, taking

in the experience with the appetite of her breed, and her own particular sensitivity.

GANDHI'S ROOM. AGA KHAN'S PALACE.
INTERIOR. DAY.

Gandhi sits by the window that is grilled rather than barred. He is spinning in a shaft of light—and looking off—as we hear a camera click and the rustle of movement. His hair, only half-gray in London, is now white.

GANDHI: Yes, I have heard of *Life Magazine.* (*A smile.*) I have even heard of Margaret Bourke-White. But I don't know why either should be interested in an old man sitting in prison when the world is blowing itself to pieces.

Bourke-White—who has been moving, crouching to shoot him and the light—sags back against the wall, relaxing at last. She has a smile as penetrating and warming as his.

BOURKE-WHITE (*a beat—and she smiles*): You're the only man I know who makes his own clothes.

Gandhi grins and glances toward his dhoti.

GANDHI: Ah, but for me that's not much of an accomplishment.

Meaning he doesn't wear many clothes. Bourke-White bursts into an appreciative radiance—already she has assessed him, and been won.

A WALL AND YARD. AGA KHAN'S PALACE.
EXTERIOR. DAY.

Gandhi walks along, Bourke-White loping along beside him, a little distance away, listening, but searching too for an angle, a moment that is right.

GANDHI: No—prison is rather agreeable to me, and there is no doubt that after the war, independence will come. My only worry is what shape it will take. Jinnah has—
BOURKE-WHITE: Stop!

She has Gandhi in the foreground, a soldier on the wall above and behind him.

BOURKE-WHITE: Now go on—just as you were.

Gandhi shrugs but suffers it. We feature him, low, from her point of view, as he walks on, the soldier pacing on the wall in the background.

BOURKE-WHITE (*coaching*): ". . . what shape it will take." Jinnah has—what?

GANDHI (*at first disconcerted, but then flowing*): Jinnah has—has cooperated with the British. It has given him power and the freedom to speak, and he has filled the Muslims with fears of what will happen to them in a country that is predominantly Hindu. (*He stops, lowering his head gravely.*) That I find hard to bear—even in prison.

She clicks.

A WALLED GARDEN IN THE PALACE. EXTERIOR. DAY.

A spinning wheel works rapidly. The camera lifts. Gandhi is at the wheel and he is smiling off at Bourke-White, who is trying ineptly to imitate him on another spinning wheel. The garden they are in has gone to seed a bit, but with latticed fretwork in the walls dappling sunlight on the grass and shrubs it is still beautiful.

BOURKE-WHITE (*archly, but emphatically of the spinning*): I do not see it as the solution to the twentieth century's problems!

She's grinning at her own frustration and she keeps trying, but there's no doubt she means it. Gandhi's smile broadens. Wryly he lifts his own "product"—a tiny roll of thread.

GANDHI: I have a friend who keeps telling me how much it costs him to keep me in poverty.

And they both laugh . . . a guard on the wall distantly looks at them wonderingly.

GANDHI (*a bit more seriously*): But I know happiness does not come with things—even twentieth century things. It can come from work, and pride in what you do. (*He looks at her steadily.*) It will not necessarily be "progress" for India if she simply imports the unhappiness of the West.

And she responds to the sophistication of that observation. He pivots around, moving beside her, and slowly demonstrates the process, taking her hands, guiding her. Bourke-white watches him as much as the wheel.

BOURKE-WHITE: But do you really believe you could use non-violence against someone like Hitler?

GANDHI (*a thoughtful pause*): Not without defeats—and great pain. (*He looks at her.*) But are there no defeats in this war—no pain? (*For a moment the thought hangs, and then Gandhi takes their hands back to the spinning.*) What you cannot do is accept injustice. From Hitler—or anyone. You must make the injustice visible—be prepared to die like a soldier to do so.

And he smiles a little wisely at her.

BOURKE-WHITE: Is my finger supposed to be wrapped around that?

GANDHI (*laughs*): No. That is what you get for distracting me.

BOURKE-WHITE: What do you expect when you talk like that?

GANDHI (*trying to unravel the mess*): I expect you to show as much patience as I am now.

His tone is not altogether patient. She looks at him in surprise and he sighs tolerantly. Then reflectively

GANDHI: Every enemy is a human being—even the worst of them. And he believes he is right and you are a beast. (*And now a little smile.*) And if you beat him over the head you will only convince him. But if you suffer, to show him that he is wrong, your sacrifice creates an atmosphere of understanding—if not with him, then in the hearts of the rest of the community on whom he depends.

Bourke-White looks at him and there is enough sense in this argument to give her pause.

GANDHI: If you are right, you will win—after much pain. (*He looks at her, then smiles in his own ironic way.*) If you are wrong, well, then, only you will suffer the blows.

She stares at him, and we know she thinks him much more profound than she had thought initially.

BA AND MIRABEHN'S ROOM. AGA KHAN'S PALACE. INTERIOR. NIGHT.

Ba, Mirabehn and Bourke-White sit on straw mats around the room, an oil lamp is the only light. It is women's talk, but Ba is defending her husband, speaking simply, but with total conviction.

BA: . . . not at all. Bapu has always said there were two kinds of slavery in India—one for women, one for the untouchables—and he has always fought against both.

Bourke-White accepts it at face value. She opens another line of inquiry.

BOURKE-WHITE: Does it rankle, being separated from him this way?

Ba pauses.

BA: Yes . . . but we see each other in the day.
BOURKE-WHITE *(delicately)*: But not at night . . .

She's terribly curious, but she doesn't want to offend. Ba sees both the curiosity and the hesitancy. She smiles acoss at Mirabehn, then

BA: In Hindu philosophy the way to God is to free yourself of possessions—and the passions that inflame to anger and jealousy. *(A smile.)* Bapu has always struggled to find the way to God.
BOURKE-WHITE: You mean he—he gave up—*(how to phrase it, finally)* married life.

Again Ba smiles.

BA: Four times he tried—and failed. *(Mirabehn and Bourke-White grin. The older woman gives a wistful smile.)* But then he took a solemn vow. . .

She shrugs . . . the implication is it was a long time ago.

BOURKE-WHITE: And he has never broken it?
BA *(a beat)*: Not yet.

She looks at them soberly and then they all burst into laughter like girls.

AGA KHAN'S PALACE. EXTERIOR. TWILIGHT.

Military move quietly but urgently in and out around the main entrance. Two military ambulances are drawn up nearby.

A British major comes down the steps quickly. He is a almost at the bottom when a British army doctor starts to go up them. The major signals him to one side. They talk quietly and confidentially.

MAJOR: I've got permission to move her—he can go too.

The doctor shakes his head.

DOCTOR: She's had a coronary throm—a serious heart failure. She wouldn't survive a trip. It's best to leave her—and hope.

The major looks defeated and depressed by the news.

BA'S ROOM. INTERIOR. TWILIGHT.

Ba lies on a mat, a pillow beneath her head, her eyes closed, her breathing short. Mirabehn sits next to her, rubbing a hand up and down her arm.

Gandhi sits a little distance away, staring at the floor and into nothingness. Pyarelal sits inconspicuously behind him.

Azad and Patel come to the doorway. Patel makes the *pranam* toward Ba and holds it as he obviously prays. Azad has bowed his head and he too is clearly making some prayer for her. Finally Azad takes just a step forward.

Gandhi looks up at him. For a moment he folds his hands absently, then he stands. He moves to Ba's side and kneels. She does not open her eyes.

GANDHI: It is time for my walk—I won't be long.

Ba's eyes flutter open. She holds her hand out to him and he takes it. When he goes to release it, she clutches it. Gandhi hesitates, and then he sits, holding Ba's hand in his lap. He looks across at Mirabehn and nods for her to go.

Mirabehn smiles weakly, gives Ba a last little rub of farewell and stands.

The doorway. Patel stands, letting Mirabehn pass before him and go down the corridor with Azad. He looks back.

His point of view. Gandhi sitting, holding Ba's hand, his eyes once more on the floor in their empty stare.

Another angle—later. The light has changed. A fly moves along a small section of the floor that still contains a ribbon of the dying sunlight.

Gandhi still sits, holding Ba's hand, staring into nothingness.

The doctor appears in the doorway. He pauses, nods amiably to Gandhi, though Gandhi does not react to his presence at all. Moving quietly, the doctor goes to the other side of Ba and crouches, and lifts her wrist to feel her pulse. He holds it for a moment, then lifts his eyes in doubt and sudden fateful apprehension. He glances at her, then slowly lowers her arm and puts the branches of his stethoscope in his ears. He puts the acoustic bell over her heart . . . a moment, and he lifts it slowly, his face confirming for us what he and we already know: there is no heartbeat. He glances at Pyarelal, who only lowers his eyes. The doctor turns his head slowly to Gandhi.

Gandhi. His point of view. His posture is utterly unchanged, Ba's hand still in his lap, his eyes still staring emptily at the floor in front of him, but suddenly tears begin to run down his cheeks. He does not move, there is no change in his empty stare, but the tears continue to flow.

A SMALL COURTYARD OF THE PALACE. EXTERIOR. DAY.

The funeral pyre burns, its work almost done.

Mirabehn, Patel, Azad, Pyarelal, stand with other prisoners and the military wardens in solemn obeisance to the dead—and the living, for Gandhi sits a little distance from the pyre, wrapped in his shawl, staring at the dying embers in tragic and impenetrable isolation as though he may never move again.

Close shot—Mirabehn watching him her face wet with tears.

DELHI AIRPORT. EXTERIOR. DAY.

Extreme close shot. A piece of cloth, shimmering in a stiff breeze . . . For a moment we hold it in silence and then we hear the sound of an aircraft growing louder and louder. And slowly the camera pulls back and we see that the cloth is part of a pennant on the nose of an aircraft.

We cut from the pennant to see the aircraft stopping before a reception area, a carpet rolled out toward its door.

An Indian regimental band strikes up martial music. A detachment of Indian Royal Air Force comes to attention at the shouted command of their NCO.

Featuring the aircraft doors. An elaborately dressed military aide opens the door and Lord Louis Mountbatten, resplendent in naval uniform, steps out onto the platform. He pauses and renders a salute.

ON A BANNERED PLATFORM.

Nehru, Lady Mountbatten and dignitaries. English and Indians watch as Mountbatten approaches a group of microphones identified as NBC, CBS, BBC, etc.

MOUNTBATTEN: We have come to crown victory with friendship— to assist at the birth of an independent India and to welcome her as an equal member in the British Commonwealth of Nations. (*A little smile.*) I am here to see that I am the last British Viceroy ever to have the honor of such a reception.

He grins in his youthful, beguiling manner and makes the *pranam* to the cheering crowd.

It is cut off by the sound of a door being opened, close.

THE GREAT PORTICO. VICE-REGAL PALACE. EXTERIOR. DAY.

Jinnah stands by one of the great pillars of the immense portico. It is a break in their Independence Conference, and as he lights a cigarette, a weary Gandhi approaches him with Azad. Jinnah's anger is clearly too deep to be left at the conference table. He slaps his lighter shut and addresses Gandhi in hushed but fiercely felt words.

JINNAH: I don't give a damn for the independence of India! I am concerned about the slavery of Muslims!

Nehru and Patel are approaching from the conference

room, both of them looking worn and angry too. Jinnah raises his voice deliberately so Nehru will hear.

JINNAH: I will not sit by to see the mastery of the British replaced by the mastery of the Hindus!

GANDHI (*patiently, not yet believing it can't be settled*): Muslim and Hindu are the right and left eye of India. No one will be slave, no one master.

Jinnah sneers at the idea, though he cools a little.

JINNAH: The world is not made of Mahatma Gandhis. (*He looks at Nehru and Patel.*) I am talking about the real world.

NEHRU: The "real India" has Muslims and Hindus in every village and every city! How do you propose to separate them?

JINNAH: Where there is a Muslim majority—that will be Pakistan. The rest is your India.

PATEL (*a forced patience*): Mohammed—the Muslims are in a majority on two different sides of the country.

JINNAH (*acidly*): Let *us* worry about Pakistan—you worry about India.

Gandhi is staring at Jinnah trying to fathom the source of his anger and fear. He turns to see that

Mountbatten has been standing in the open door to the conference room, as torn as Gandhi by the conflict, feeling it best controlled in formal discussion.

MOUNTBATTEN: Gentlemen, perhaps we should recommence.

Gandhi nods, and reluctantly the adversaries move back to the conference room. Gandhi is last through the door. He pauses by Mountbatten, a little sigh—"How difficult, how difficult"—then he puts a friendly hand on Mountbatten's shoulder and the two of them enter together.

GANDHI'S ASHRAM. EXTERIOR. DAY.

Featuring Godse waving a black flag and shouting.

GODSE (*with others*): Death to Jinnah! Death to Jinnah!

We have pulled back and we see a whole gathering of Hindu youths near the entrance to the ashram. Many wave black flags. A couple of trucks that have brought them, and a car, are along the path. Kallenbach is stepping out of an old 1942 open Austin that he has put in a waiting position near the entrance to the path. The chanting shout "Death to Jinnah!" suddenly dies. The youths—and Kallenbach— look back toward the ashram.

Featuring Gandhi's bungalow. Nehru has stepped out onto the porch and he glares at the youths. It is his presence that has silenced them.

Kallenbach smiles.

GANDHI'S BUNGALOW. INTERIOR. DAY.

Gandhi is rising from the floor, where his spinning wheel sits. He stops, halfway up, listening, then, a weary sigh.

GANDHI: Thank God, they've stopped.

Mirabehn is spinning across the room. She lifts her head as a signal to someone out of shot.

Gandhi's two grand nieces, Manu and Abha, who help Mirabehn now that Ba is gone, rise quickly at Mirabehn's signal, Manu to help with his shawl, Abha to hold his sandals so that he can slip into them.

GANDHI: I'm your grand uncle but I can still walk either of you into the ground and I don't need to be pampered this way!

It's cross—he's worried about other things. Mirabehn just smiles at it. Gandhi looks down at Abha, and taps her sharply on the top of the head.

GANDHI: Finish your quota of spinning.

She nods obediently, the flicker of a smile around her mouth, youthful, irrepressible. The beauty of it almost saddens Gandhi. He taps her again—gently—and goes out.

GANDHI'S ASHRAM. EXTERIOR. DAY.

Kallenbach shoos a chicken from the back seat of the Austin and dusts off the seat. He steps back out.

Gandhi is approaching with Nehru and Azad, Pyaralel trails close behind. We have seen Azad and Pyaralel come out on the porch behind Nehru. As Gandhi nears the car a Hindu youth with a black flag calls to him.

HINDU YOUTH: Bapu—please. Don't do it!

They are all awed, timid even in his actual presence, and the mood of their gathering has changed altogether. Gandhi looks at the youth and the line of others.

GANDHI *(impatiently)*: What do you want me not to do? Not to meet with Mr. Jinnah? *(Fiercely)* I am a Muslim! *(He stares at them, then relents.)* And a Hindu, and a Christian and a Jew— and so are all of you. When you wave those flags and shout you send fear into the hearts of your brothers.

He sweeps them sternly with his eyes, all his fatigue and strain showing.

GANDHI: That is not the India I want. Stop it. For God's sake, stop it.

And he lowers his head and moves on to the car, where Kallenbach holds the door for him, Nehru, Azad and Pyar- alal following.
Another angle. As they get into the car, we see the car that sits by the two trucks that have brought the youths. In the back seat we see two men, one of whom is Prakash (The bearded man at Gandhi's assassination).

JINNAH'S DRAWING ROOM. INTERIOR. NIGHT.

Jinnah is on the small balcony of this elaborate room. He is looking down in a slightly supercilious manner. As usual he is impeccably dressed.

JINNAH: Now, please, if you've finished your prayers, could we begin with business.

He has been looking at
Gandhi, who sits on the floor of the large room some distance from him, just lifting his head from prayers.
Nehru, Patel and Azad are on the same side of the room as Gandhi. They rise from prayer as Jinnah comes down the steps to them. Gandhi hesitates, then begins.

GANDHI: My dear Jinnah, you and I are brothers born of the same Mother India. If you have fears, I want to put them to rest. *(Jinnah listens impatiently, sceptically. Gandhi just glances in Nehru's direction.)* I am asking Panditji to stand down. I want you to be the first Prime Minister of India *(Jinnah raises an eyebrow of interest.)*—to name your entire cabinet, to make the head of every government department a Muslim.

And Jinnah has drawn himself up. His vanity is too great not to be touched by that prospect. He measures Gandhi for a moment to see that he is sincere, and when he is satisfied with that, he turns slowly to Nehru, Patel and Azad.

Nehru glances at Patel. They have all been taken by surprise by the offer—and do not feel what Gandhi feels. Nehru looks hesitantly at Gandhi.

NEHRU: Bapu, for me, and the rest *(his hand gestures to Patel and Azad)*, if that is what you want, we will accept it. But out there *(he indicates the streets)* already there is rioting beause Hindus fear you are going to give too much away.

PATEL: If you did this, no one could control it. No one.

It bears the stamp of undeniable truth. Gandhi's eyes sag with the despair of a man whose last hope, whose faith, has crumbled around him.

Jinnah smiles cynically, he spreads his hands "See?"

JINNAH: It is your choice. Do you want an independent India and an independent Pakistan? Or do you want civil war?

Gandhi stares at him numbly.

THE RED FORT. NEW DELHI. EXTERIOR. DAY.

On a platform in the foreground Mountbatten and Nehru. A band plays the Indian National Anthem loudly and there is the roar of a tremendous crowd as the green, white and saffron flag of India is raised on the flagpole.

GOVERNMENT BUILDING. KARACHI.
EXTERIOR. DAY.

On a platform in the foreground Jinnah and a British plenipotentiary. A band plays the new Pakistani National Anthem loudly and there is the roar of a tremendous crowd as the white, green with white crescent, flag of Pakistan is raised on the flagpole.

THE ASHRAM. EXTERIOR. DAY.

Silence. The little flagpole is empty, the rope dangling, flapping loosely down the pole.

Gandhi sits on the porch of his bungalow, spinning. The hum of the spinning wheel. Inside we can just see Mira-behn, spinning too. But apart from that, he is alone; the whole ashram seems deserted. We hear the sound of a bell on one of the goats, fairly distant.

THE PATH TO THE ASHRAM. EXTERIOR. DAY.

Featuring Kallenbach. He is taking the goat and tether-ing it near the path of the ashram. He stills the bell with his hand. As he ties it the camera angle widens and we see Margaret Bourke-White sitting on the grass, watching Kal-lenbach and looking off toward Gandhi's bungalow.

BOURKE-WHITE: Aren't you being a little overprotective?

Kallenbach looks at her. Her tone criticizes more than his stilling the goat's bell.

KALLENBACH: Tomorrow. Tomorrow photograph him.
BOURKE-WHITE: I came all this way because I believed the picture of Independence Day was of him here alone.

Kallenbach stands and looks across at her, judging, then appealing to her humanity.

KALLENBACH: It is violence, and the fear of violence, that have made today what it is. . . Give him the dignity of his grief.

Bourke-White grabs a clump of grass, twists it free, and sighs. She tosses the grass vaguely at the goat.

BOURKE-WHITE: And while we're sitting here feeding goats, what will happen to all the Muslims in India and the Hindus in Pakistan?

Kallenbach stops, staring absently at the ground ahead, then

KALLENBACH: Gandhi will pray for them. . .

OPEN TERRAIN AND RAILROAD. EXTERIOR. DAY.

The camera is high (helicopter) and moving and from its position we meet and then pass over an immense column of refugees—ten, twenty abreast—moving down one side of the railroad track toward camera. Women, children, the sick, the aged, all burdened with bedding, utensils, household treasures, useless bric-a-brac and trudging with them every type of cart, wagon, rickshaw, pulled by donkey, camel, bike, oxen. It stretches endlessly to the horizon. Tiny green, white and saffron flags here and there indicate that it is a Hindu column and spotted through it we see people in fresh bandages, some on stretchers, sticking out like radioactive tracers in the huge artery of frightened humanity.

And the camera lifts and tilts, slowly swinging to the opposite direction, and as it does, reveals another vast column across the track, several yards away, moving in the opposite direction: veiled women in purdah, the crescent flag of Muslim Pakistan here and there. As the camera levels and speeds along it, we see that this column too reaches to the horizon, that it too carries its wounded.

An unbelieveable flood of desperate humanity.

EXTREME CLOSE SHOT.

The sound of the vast refugee column. A woman's arms cradle a baby in swaddling. Blood has seeped through the swaddling in three or four places, some of it dried. Flies buzz around it. And suddenly we hear the woman's sobs and she rocks the baby and we know it has stopped moving, stopped breathing, and a male hand gently touches the back of the baby, checking, and the camera pans up to the face of a man.

Again in extreme close shot so we cannot tell whether they are Hindu or Muslim. And the man's eyes knot, and he swings out of shot as he runs in fury and rage at the other column.

LONG SHOT. HIGH.

The two columns—and a howl of hate and grief! And the camera sweeps to where men are running at each other across the track, some already fighting. Knives, pangas, hatchets; women screaming and running; a beseiged wagon tipped.

Another angle. And as the fighting grows more fierce streams of men from each column run back to partake, but the bulk of the two columns hurries off, scrambling, running, some leaving their burdens, fleeing the meleé in terror.

HINDU/MUSLIM RIOT SEQUENCE. SEVERAL LOCATIONS. DAY/NIGHT.

A Muslim pulled through broken glass in an urban market shop./Night: a hindu temple daubed with blood, the bodies of women and children strewn before it; screams, the sound of fighting./ Mud and straw houses burning, figures running through them./ A city street: a truck crashes into a barricade of rickshaws and bales, and is set upon by a swarm of knife- and panga-bearing men. From the back of the truck opponents with swords and clubs leap into battle.

NEHRU'S OFFICE. INTERIOR. DAY.

Chaos. It and the adjoining office have been made into something like operations rooms. Military and civilian aides move back and forth. Telephones at work everywhere. A huge map on the wall is constantly having data changed by people receiving messages there.

Nehru is glancing at a telex message; he turns and gives it back to the military aide who's given it to him.

NEHRU (curt, fast): No. There just are not that many troops.
MILITARY AIDE: What's he to do?
NEHRU: What he can!

He turns. Patel has a message he was going to present to him. He hesitates, grins dismally, and crumples the message—"No use." Nehru sags. He looks at Patel with haggard eyes.

NEHRU: He was right. It's insane—anything would have been better.
PATEL: Have you found him?

Nehru nods solemnly.

NEHRU: He's in Noakhali.

Patel reacts to that—surprise, apprehension.

NEHRU: He's tramping from village to village—no police, no troops—trying to quell the madness single-handedly. (*He sighs, half in admiration, half in hopeless exasperation at the old man's audacity.*) Maulana has gone to bring him back.

Patel nods grimly—the noisy chaos of the room. Someone shouts at Nehru, "Prime Minister!"

CLOSE SHOT. GANDHI.

In silence—looking tragic, tired and defeated. He is sitting in his characteristic manner, staring down at the carpet before him.

NEHRU'S VOICE (*dull, lifeless*): What you have done in Noakhali is a miracle, Bapu, a, miracle, but millions are on the move—millions. There is no way to stop it . . . and no one can count the dead.

The camera angle has changed. We are in

NEHRU'S PRIVATE CHAMBERS. INTERIOR. NIGHT.

Patel and Azad are there and Pyarelal of course, and with them now the giant figure of Abdul Ghaffar Khan, the first time we have seen him among Gandhi's intimate group.

NEHRU: In Calcutta it's like civil war. The Muslims rose and there was a bloodbath, and now the Hindus are taking revenge—and if we can't stop it there'll be no hope for the Hindus left in Pakistan.

PATEL: . . . an eye for an eye making the whole world blind.

It is an empty and despairing echo of Gandhi's words.

AZAD: Aren't there any troops to spare?

NEHRU (*tense, fragile*): Nothing—nothing. The divisions in Bombay and Delhi can hardly keep the peace now. And each fresh bit of news creates another wave of mad . . . ness.

He has turned and seen Gandhi standing slowly. It has almost stopped him.

PATEL: Could we cut all news off? I know—
NEHRU: Bapu—please. Where are you going?
GANDHI (*sounding like an old man*): I don't want to hear more. . .

He is moving toward the door. It stops them all. Pyarelal moves tentatively to open the door.

PATEL (*impatiently*): We need your help!
GANDHI: There is nothing I can give.
AZAD: Where are you going?

Gandhi turns, looks at him bleakly.

GANDHI: Calcutta.

CALCUTTA. EXTERIOR. NIGHT.

We are high. There are fires, the sounds of spasmodic gunfire, of looting, screams, the roar of police vehicles and occasional sirens. The camera zooms in on a poor quarter of artisan dwellings in narrow streets. Outside one of the houses is a car, an army jeep, policemen, a few soldiers and a group of people. It seems a little inland of calm in a sea of wild chaos.

On the roof of the house, a figure moves into the light.

CLOSER. TAHIB'S ROOF.

The figure is Gandhi. He peers down at the dark, rioting streets. Azad, Tahib, a Muslim whose house this is, Mirabehn and Pyarelal are with him along with Abdul Ghaffar Khan.

A police commissioner moves to Gandhi's side, demanding his attention.

POLICE COMMISSIONER: Sir, please, I don't have the men to protect you—not in a Muslim house. Not this quarter.
GANDHI: I am staying with the friend of a friend.

There is a sudden commotion just below them and angry shouts: "Death to Muslims!," "Death to Muslims!"
Gandhi peers down.
His point of view. A surging gang of youths, many carry-

ing torches, and far outnumbering the little group of police and soldiers, are shouting up at the roof. We see three or four black flags and stains of blood on many of them. A few hold knives still wet with blood.

A YOUTH: There he is!

A feral roar goes up at the sight of Gandhi, but he stands unmoving.

HINDU YOUTH LEADER (*his voice emotional, tearful*): Why are you staying at the home of a Muslim! They're murderers! They killed my family!

Featuring Gandhi. It is a comment too grave for glibness, and Gandhi is obviously struck by the pain of it. He pauses for a moment, staring down at the youth:

GANDHI: Because forgiveness is the gift of the brave.

He makes it mean the youth. For a second it makes an impact, but then the youth shouts his defiance at him and his message.

YOUTH: To hell with you, Gandhi!!

An angry chorus of acclamation; when it dies

GANDHI (*to the youth*): Go—do as your mother and father would wish you to do.

It is ambiguous, open-ended, meaning anything your mother and father would wish you to do. Tears flush from the boy's eyes and he stares at Gandhi with a kind of hopeless anguish and rage. But the impact is on the youth alone; around him the others begin to take up the chant "Death to Muslims!," "Death to Muslims!"

Gandhi turns from the street. He looks at the police commissioner—at his fatigue, his concern, his manifest respect. Gandhi musters a weary smile.

GANDHI: I have lived a lifetime. If I had shunned death—or feared it—I would not be here. Nor would you be concerned for me. (*He lets it sinks in then he takes the commissioner's arm and moves back toward the center of the roof*). Leave me—and take your men. (*An understanding touch of the arm.*) You have more important things to worry about.

The commissioner looks at him, uncertain, not knowing what to do, as the angry chanting continues above the sound of rioting.

HOSPITAL. INTERIOR. DAY.

An old, inadequate hospital—dark, cavernous. Margaret Bourke-White is moving among the densely packed litter of wounded women. She is positioning herself to photograph Gandhi, who is speaking to a woman who cradles a small baby. The corridors behind him are even more packed. The few doctors and nurses hardly have room to move.

Featuring Gandhi. Azad and Mirabehn are behind him as he moves on, and behind them, like a giant guardian, Abdul Ghaffar Khan. We hear "Bapu, Bapu" muttered quietly here and there. Gandhi bends to a woman whose face is bandaged and a cruel wound is half-exposed between her mouth and her eye.

WOMAN: Bapu . . . Allah be with you . . .

There are tears in Gandhi's eyes now.

GANDHI: And with you. (*He touches her wrinkled hand.*) Pray . . . I cannot help you—pray . . . pray.

And the weight of his helplessness hangs on him.

CALCUTTA STREET. EXTERIOR. DAY.

A streetcar (tram) crashes into a barricade of carts, rick-shaws, a couple of old cars, smashing through to breach the barricade, but stopped in the end by the mass of debris. The streetcar is loaded with Indian troops and they break from the stalled vehicle to chase

A gang of Hindus—organized—runs down the street from the troops, some dragging the bodies of victims with them. We see several Hindu black flags.

NEHRU'S OFFICE. INTERIOR. NIGHT.

He speaks across his desk to a senior police commissioner. The same activity going on in the background.

NEHRU (*angrily*): No! There will not be a Hindu Police and a Muslim Police. There is one police!

An aide slips a newspaper on his desk in front of him. He doesn't look at it till the senior police commissioner lowers his head and turns, accepting defeat. Then Nehru glances at the paper.

In thick headlines: GANDHI: A FAST UNTO DEATH!

Nehru doesn't move for a moment. Then he lifts his face slowly to his aide.

NEHRU: Why must I read news like this in the paper?

The aide shakes his head—there's no answer. Nehru lowers his head again; it is like another burden on a man who already has too many. He grips his temples . . . a terrible sigh.

NEHRU: Tell Patel. Arrange a plane. We will go—Friday.

THE AIDE: Four days?

Nehru thinks on it solemnly, then nods yes.

TAHIB'S HOUSE. EXTERIOR. DAY.

The sounds of rioting and looting on nearby streets, but here a mass of people are gathered. Many youths with black flags. Two black government limousines. Motorcycles. Police and soldiers. They are looking off to

AN OUTSIDE STAIRCASE. TAHIB'S HOUSE

It runs up the side of the building and is lined with waiting people. Nehru and Patel are climbing the stairs, moving past them almost irritably as they mutter "Nehru, Nehru," "Patel," and make the *pranam* to the eminent men.

In the heat of the city Tahib's rooftop is still Gandhi's "home" and has become a center of activity. Azad clears someone aside and ushers Nehru and Patel under the canopy awning.

Nehru pauses as he lowers his head.

His point of view. Gandhi lies curled awkwardly on his side on the cot. He is writing, Pyarelal taking the pages as he finishes, both ignoring all the people, the sounds of gunfire and distant shouting, but he looks tired and tightens his jaw occasionally in pain. The camera pans. A doctor sits near the foot of the cot, Abdul Ghaffar Khan beyond him. Near the other edge of the canopied area, Mirabehn sits with Bourke-White. They are whispering quietly, but Mirabehn has stopped on seeing Nehru and she smiles a relieved greeting. She knows Gandhi's feeling for him. Bourke-White stares at him and Patel for a second and then her hand goes slowly, almost reflexively, for her camera.

CLOSER ON GANDHI.

Nehru crosses and kneels so that he is almost at Gandhi's eyeline. Gandhi must take his eyes from his writing to look, and he is almost moved to tears at the sight of Nehru. His hand shakes a little as he holds it out to him.

NEHRU: Bapu . . .

Gandhi turns to pat their joined hands with his other hand. He does so with effort, and at last he sees Patel.

GANDHI: Sardar . . . (He looks him over.) You have gained weight. You must join me in the fast.

Patel sits near the head of the cot so the three of them are on a level. Outside the canopied area, Bourke-White is crouched, her camera framing the three of them.

PATEL (wittily, warmly): If I fast I die. If you fast people go to all sorts of trouble to keep you alive.

Gandhi smiles and reaches to touch hands with him.

NEHRU: Bapu, forgive me—I've cheated. I could have come earlier. But your fast has helped. These last days people's minds have begun to turn to this bed—and away from last night's atrocity. But now it is enough.

Gandhi shakes his head.

GANDHI: All that has happened is that I've grown a little thinner.

It is despairingly sincere. But Nehru feels he has an antidote for that despair. The distant sound of an explosion.

NEHRU: Tomorrow five thousand Muslim students of all ages are marching here in Calcutta—for peace. *(The real point)* And five thousand Hindu students ae marching with them. It is all organized.

Bourke-White captures the sense of elation in his face. From her discreet distance, she lowers the camera, holding it against her mouth, waiting for Gandhi's response.

Gandhi nods to Nehru, accepting the news with a sad wistfulness.

GANDHI: I'm glad—but it will not be enough.

Nehru isn't prepared for this resistance. He glances at Patel, and we see that they recognize that their bland conviction that they could talk him out of the fast was deeply misplaced. Nehru turns back—this time no confidence, only concern. A forced smile.

NEHRU: Bapu, you are not so young anymore.

Gandhi smiles, pain etched in his eyes. He touches Nehru's hand.

GANDHI: Don't worry for me—death will be a deliverance. *(There is water in his eyes, but his words have the weight of a man truly determined to die.)* I cannot watch the destruction of all I have lived for.

Nehru stares at him, feeling the sudden fear that Gandhi means it. Patel, Mirabehn, Azad, Bourke-White are gripped by the same realization.

TAHIB'S HOUSE. EXTERIOR. NIGHT.

An outside broadcast truck is parked among the usual crowd, grown even larger now, and more women among them. The sounds of distant fighting.

TAHIB'S ROOF. EXTERIOR. NIGHT.

The senior technician, in earphones, signals across to Mirabehn. She holds a microphone by Gandhi, who is lying on his side. He seems almost out of touch.

MIRABEHN: Bapu . . .

Gandhi looks at her, and then the microphone. When he speaks into the microphone his voice is very weak.

GANDHI: Each night before I sleep, I read a few words from the Gita and the Koran, and the Bible . . . *(we intercut with Bourke-White and those on the roof watching)* tonight I ask you to share these thoughts of God with me.

And now we go out into the streets, intercutting with Gandhi but seeing Hindus listening around loudspeakers on corners, in little eating houses, Muslim shops where people live in the back, and neighbors gathering defensively in groups.

GANDHI *(the books are there, but he does it from memory of course)*: I will begin with the Bible where the words of the Lord are, "Love thy neighbor as thyself" . . . and then our beloved Gita which says, "The world is a garment worn by God, thy neighbor is in truth thyself" . . . and finally the Holy Koran, "We shall remove all hatred from our hearts and recline on couches face to face, a band of brothers."

He leans back, exhausted. Mirabehn is looking at him; she starts to sing softly.

MIRABEHN: "Lead Kindly Light, amidst the circling gloom . . ."

Gandhi, his eyes closed, takes it up in his weak, croaking voice.

GANDHI/MIRABEHN: "The night is dark, and I am far from home, Lead thou me on . . ."

TAHIB'S HOUSE. EXTERIOR. DAY.

Two police motorcycles lead a black limousine to a stop before Tahib's house. The crowd now gathered is very large. More mixed than before but still predominantly of youths, many still with black flags.

Nehru gets out of the limousine with a Muslim leader, a tough-looking man who carries himself with the authority and power of a mobster (Suhrawardy). And they start to go up the outside stairs.

Suddenly we hear the shout "Death to Gandhi!," "Death to Gandhi!" And Nehru turns, pushing past Suhrawardy fiercely and going back onto the street. He runs at the crowd, where the shout comes once more from the back. His face is wild with anger and shock.

NEHRU (*hysterically*): Who dares say such things! Who?! (*And he is running at them and they spread in fear.*) Come! Kill me first! Come! Where are you?! Kill me first!

The crowd has spread from him all along the street; they stand against the walls of the houses staring at him, terrified to move. We see, just in passing, the frightened, apprehensive faces of Godse, and near him, Apte and Karkare.

Nehru stands, staring at them all, his face seething with anger.

TAHIB'S ROOF. EXTERIOR. DAY.

We are featuring a copy of *Life Magazine*. On the cover is a picture of rioting men fighting and diagonally a cut-out of Gandhi lying on his cot. The caption reads: "An Old Man's Battle." As the magazine starts to be opened, it is suddenly put to one side.

Another angle. Mirabehn is rising, leaving the magazine at her feet. She moves to Nehru and Suhrawardy as Azad ushers them into the canopied area. Abdul Ghaffar Khan sits quietly in the background. Mirabehn speaks softly.

MIRABEHN: His pulse is very irregular—the kidneys aren't functioning.

Nehru looks across at Gandhi. The doctor, who is testing Gandhi's pulse yet again, glances at him—no encouragement—and moves away. Nehru moves to the side of the cot and Gandhi smiles weakly and holds out a hand, but he is in pain.

NEHRU: Bapu, I have brought Mr. Suhrawardy. It was he who called on the Muslims to rise; he is telling them now to go back to their homes, to lay down their arms.

Gandhi looks up at Suhrawardy, who nods. Gandhi looks back at Nehru. There is no hint of him changing his mind.

NEHRU (*personally*): Think what you can do by living—that you cannot do by dying.

Gandhi smiles whimsically, he touches him again but there is no change in his attitude.

NEHRU (*pleadingly*): What do you want?

GANDHI (*a moment*): That the fighting will stop—that you make me believe it will never start again.

Nehru looks at him hopelessly.

A SQUARE IN CALCUTTA. EXTERIOR. DAY.

A huge crowd, some smoke in distant buildings, some damage near to help us know this is still Calcutta, and all is not yet at peace. The camera sweeps over the crowd, past the loudspeakers on their poles. We see surly knots of belligerent rowdies, mostly young, but not all, hanging on the fringes as we move over the heads of the mass of listening people to a platform where Nehru speaks. Azad, Suhrawardy, and others sit on the floor behind him. We have heard his voice over all this.

NEHRU: . . . Sometimes it is when you are quite without hope and in utter darkness that God comes to the rescue. Gandhiji is dying because of our madness. Put away your "revenge." What will be gained by more killing? Have the courage to do what you know is right. For God's sake, let us embrace like brothers . . .

TAHIB'S ROOF. EXTERIOR. NIGHT.

Featuring the Muslim leader Suhrawardy, leaning against a wall, watching an action out of shot with evident tension. We hear a little clank of metal.

Another angle. There are five men facing Gandhi. They wear black trousers and black knit vests. There are thongs around their arms that make their bulging muscles seem even more powerful. They are Hindu thugs (Goondas). Their clothes are dirty—and they are too—but they are laying knives and guns at Gandhi's feet.

Mirabehn, Azad, Pyarelal, the doctor and others on the roof watch fascinated, a little frightened.

GOONDA LEADER: It is our promise. We stop. It is a promise.

Gandhi is looking at him, testing, not giving or accepting anything that is mere gesture.

GANDHI: Go—try—God be with you.

The Goondas stand. They glance at Suhrawardy; he smiles tautly and they start to leave, but one (Nahari) lingers. Suddenly he moves violently toward Gandhi, taking a flat piece of Indian bread *(chapati)* from his trousers and tossing it forcefully on Gandhi.

NAHARI: Eat.

Mirabehn and Azad start to move toward him—the man looks immensely strong and immensely unstable. But Gandhi holds up a shaking hand, stopping them. Nahari's face is knotted in emotion, half anger, half almost a child's fear— but there is a wild menace in that instability.

NAHARI: Eat! I am going to hell—but not with your death on my soul.

GANDHI: Only God decides who goes to hell . . .

NAHARI *(stiffening, aggressive)*: I—I killed a child. . . . *(Then an anguished defiance)* I smashed his head against a wall.

Gandhi stares at him, breathless.

GANDHI *(in a fearful whisper)*: Why? Why?

It is as though the man has told him of some terrible self-inflicted wound.

NAHARI *(tears now—and wrath)*: They killed my son—my boy!

Almost reflexively he holds his hand out to indicate the height of his son. He glares at Suhrawardy and then back at Gandhi.

NAHARI: The Muslims killed my son . . . they killed him.

He is sobbing, but in his anger it seems almost as though he means to kill Gandhi in retaliation. A long moment, as Gandhi meets his pain and wrath. Then

GANDHI: I know a way out of hell.

Nahari sneers, but there is just a flicker of desperate curiosity.

GANDHI: Find a child—a child whose mother and father have been killed. A little boy—about this high.

He raises his hand to the height Nahari has indicated as his son's.

GANDHI: . . . and raise him—as your own.

Nahari has listened. His face almost cracks—it is a chink of light, but it does not illumine his darkness.

GANDHI: Only be sure . . . that he is a Muslim. And that you raise him as one.

And now the light falls on Nahari. His face stiffens, he swallows, fighting any show of emotion; then he turns to go. But he takes only a step and he turns back, going to his knees, the sobs breaking again and again from his heaving body as he holds his head to Gandhi's feet in the traditional greeting of Hindu son to Hindu father. A second, and Gandhi reaches out and touches the top of his head.

Mirabehn watches. The Goondas watch. Suhrawardy watches. Finally

GANDHI (gently, exhaustedly): Go—go. God bless you . . .

COURTYARD. POLICE STATION. CALCUTTA. EXTERIOR. NIGHT.

Trucks with riot squads (shields and truncheons) in place, but they are lounging, waiting. There is silence, an air of somnolence. Some of the riot squad lounge in little groups around the courtyard. A distant cough.

Featuring a senior riot squad officer dressed and ready for action. He it is who coughed. He coughs again, clearing his throat. A police sergeant stands by him, both are reading the front page of a paper the senior riot squad officer holds. We see two huge lines of headline: GANDHI NEAR DEATH/ NEHRU GOES ON FAST.

In one of the trucks one of the men offers another a cigarette.

A telephone rings sharply, inside. The senior riot squad officer and the sergeant run in as engines start; the men run to their places, lower visors, headlights go on!

POLICE STATION OFFICE. INTERIOR. DAY.

A constable mans the telephone. He listens as the senior riot squad officer and the sergeant run to him tensely. The sound of the great doors opening in the courtyard, more engines revving up.

CONSTABLE: Yes, sir, yes, sir, *(He holds up his hand to the senior officer)* "Wait."

He glances up at the senior riot squad officer.

CONSTABLE *(writing, from the phone)*: Accident, "Christie cross-roads," a lorry and a rickshaw. Yes, sir, I have it.

He shrugs at the senior riot squad officer and hands the information slip to another constable behind the desk.

The sergeant sighs, and moves to the outside door. We hear him bellow, "Stand down." The constable hangs up and sighs heavily. The senior riot squad officer shakes his head, and turns and walks slowly to the door.

COURTYARD. POLICE STATION. EXTERIOR. NIGHT.

The senior riot squad officer and the sergeant stand in the doorway as the engines die. The men relax . . . the silence returns. A dog barks distantly, disturbed by the noise. . . A bird caws once or twice.

SERGEANT: I wouldn't have believed it, Mr. Gupta.
SENIOR OFFICER: Sergeant, it's a bloody miracle. . .

HIGH SHOT. CALCUTTA. EXTERIOR. NIGHT.

It lies in silence.

TAHIB'S ROOF. EXTERIOR. DAY.

Mirabehn is bent over Gandhi. He is curled almost in the fetal position, his face looking wan and sunken. For the first time there is silence, no explosions, no distant shouts, no gunfire.

MIRABEHN: Bapu, there's been no fighting—anywhere. It has stopped—the madness has stopped.

We see the police commissioner, Suhrawardy, two doctors, Abdul Ghaffar Khan, and some others. Nearer Gandhi, behind Mirabehn, are Nehru, Patel, Azad and Pyarelal.

Gandhi turns to Mirabehn, his face shaking, peering into her eyes.

GANDHI: It is foolish if it is just to save the life of an old man.

MIRABEHN: No . . . no. In every temple and mosque they have pledged to die before they lift a hand against each other.

His weary eyes look at her; he looks up slowly to Azad. Azad nods "It's true." Then Patel

PATEL: Everywhere.

Gandhi looks at Nehru. Nehru just nods tautly. Gandhi looks down, then lifts his head to Azad.

GANDHI: Maulana, my friend, could I have some orange juice. . . Then you and I will take a piece of bread together. . .

The relief brings water to their eyes and grins to their faces. Nehru bends to Gandhi. Gandhi holds his hand out to him, and Nehru clutches it. Then

NEHRU: You see, Bapu, it is not difficult. I have fasted only a few hours and I accomplished what you could not do in as many days.

It is a joke in their way with each other and Gandhi's eyes light, his smile comes. But it is tired. He puts his other hand over Nehru's and Nehru lowers his head to it, crying silently.

BIRLA HOUSE. EXTERIOR. DAY.

As in the opening sequence—but a few minutes earlier. The crowd is beginning to gather for the evening prayers. We see a tonga or two, a gardener opening the gate to the garden, three policemen standing, talking idly among themselves.

BIRLA HOUSE. INTERIOR. DAY.

Laughter. Gandhi is eating *muli*; he holds his head back to capture the lemon juice. We hear the click of a camera.

GANDHI: That is how you eat *muli.*

Manu hands him a cloth and he wipes his hands. Another click of a camera. He is not fully recovered, but well on the way.

GANDHI *(to the photographer)*: I'm not sure I want to be remembered that way.

It is all light and for fun. We get a wide-angle shot now and see that Bourke-White is shooting one of her favorite subjects again. She is enjoying the banter, as is Mirabehn, who is spinning quietly to one side of the room, and Patel, who sits cross-legged like Gandhi on the floor. Pyarelal is working on papers with him but grins at this.

BOURKE-WHITE: Don't worry, with luck you may not be.

And she shoots him again, as he hands the cloth back to Manu. Abha is sitting next to Manu, looking at a collection of pictures of Gandhi, obviously Bourke-White's.

PATEL: No, he'll be remembered for tempting fate.

It is wry, but waspishly chiding. Abha suddenly holds a picture up for Gandhi to see. It's one of him, ears wide, eyes round.

ABHA: Mickey Mouse.

Gandhi taps her on the head with his finger as she smiles. But Bourke-White has looked from Patel to Gandhi, clearly shaken by the implication in Patel's words.

BOURKE-WHITE: You really are going to Pakistan, then? *(Gandhi shrugs, and she chides too)* You *are* a stubborn man.

GANDHI *(a grin, in the mood of their "flirtation")*: I'm simply going to prove to Muslims there, and Hindus here, that the only devils in the world are those running around in our own hearts—and that's where all our battles ought to be fought.

Abha has signaled to the cheap watch dangling from his dhoti. He glances at it, and holds his arms out. The two girls help him.

BOURKE-WHITE: And what kind of a warrior have you been in that warfare?

She is photographing his getting-up and leaning on the two girls.

GANDHI: Not a very good one. That's why I have so much tolerance for the other scoundrels of the world.

He moves off, but has a sudden thought and turns to Patel.

GANDHI: Ask Panditji to—to consider what we've discussed.

Patel nods soberly and Gandhi starts for the door, Bourke-White moving with him.

GANDHI (*of the photographs*): Enough.
BOURKE-WHITE (*a plea*): One more.

He has passed her, he's in the doorway. We see the crowd at the end of the garden, where the light of the day is beginning to soften. He turns, teasing in his slightly flirtatious way with women.

GANDHI: You're a temptress.

She shoots him against the door—the crowd milling distantly, waiting—then she lowers her camera.

BOURKE-WHITE: Just an admirer . . .
GANDHI: Nothing's more dangerous, especially for an old man.

He turns; the last words have betrayed the smile on his face; they have a painful sense of truth about them. Bourke-White watches as he moves into the garden toward the crowd in the distance.
She turns to Mirabehn.

BOURKE-WHITE: There's a sadness in him.

It's an observation—and a question. Mirabehn accedes gravely.

MIRABEHN: He thinks he's failed.

Bourke-White stares at her, then turns to look out at him.

BOURKE-WHITE: Why? My God, if anything's proved him right, it's a what's happened these last months. . .

Mirabehn nods, but she keeps on spinning and tries to sound cynically resigned but her innate emotionalism keeps breaking through in her voice and on her face.

MIRABEHN: I am blinded by my love of him, but I think when we most needed it, he offered the world a way out of madness. But he doesn't see it . . . and neither does the world.

It is laced with pain. Bourke-White turns and looks out at Gandhi—so tiny, so weak as he walks between his "props." He has now reached the end of the garden and is moving among the crowd assembled there.

THE GARDEN. BIRLA HOUSE.
EXTERIOR. TWILIGHT.

Gandhi is moving forward in the crowd, one hand resting on Manu, the other on Abha. He makes the *pranam* to someone, the crowd is bowing to him, some speaking, and we also see the crowd from his point of view—"Bapu," "God bless you," "Thank you—thank you." He turns to a very old woman, who makes a salaam to him. Gandhi touches her head.

GANDHI: Allah be with you.

Smiling, he turns back. A jostling, the sound of beads falling.

MANU *(to someone)*: Brother, Bapu is already late for prayers.

Gandhi turns to the person; he makes the *pranam.*
Full shot. Godse is making the *pranam* to him and he suddenly, wildly draws his gun and fires. The camera closes on Gandhi as he staggers and falls, the red stain of blood seeping through his white shawl.

GANDHI: Oh, God . . . oh, God . . .

Manu and Abha bend over him, silent in their first shock. The sound of panic and alarm begins to grow around them, they suddenly scream and begin to cry.

MANU/ABHA: Bapu! Bapu!

A FUNERAL PYRE. EXTERIOR. DAY.

Blackness. Silence.

A moment—we sense the blackness moving—like dark smoke.

The camera is pulling back very slowly and we can tell the blackness is smoke rising from a fire.

And now we see that it is a funeral pyre. And all around that pyre a mass of silent humanity. Through the smoke, sitting cross-legged near the rim of the flames, we see Nehru . . . and Azad and Patel, Mirabehn and Kallenbach, the drawn faces of Lord and Lady Mountbatten, Manu and Abha . . .

THE RIVER. EXTERIOR. DAY.

A helicopter shot coming slowly up the wide river, low, toward a barge and a mass of people in the distance.

And now we are over the barge, and it is covered with flowers. Flowers flow downstream around it. An urn sits on it—containing Gandhi's ashes—and Nehru stands near it, Azad and Patel a little behind him. And as the barge floats down the river, Nehru bends and lifts the urn. . .

Featuring Nehru. He swallows, restraining his own emotion, and slowly, ritualistically, sprinkles the ashes over the water.

And as they spread, we hold on that stretch of the river, the flowers swirling languidly around it as the dark, timeless current moves them toward the sea.

GANDHI'S VOICE (*weak, struggling, as he spoke the words to Mirabehn*): . . . There have been tyrants and murderers—and for a time they can seem invincible. But in the end they always fall. Think of it—always . . . When you are in doubt that that is God's way, the way the world is meant to be . . . think of that.

And slowly the camera begins pulling back, leaving the flowers, the brown, rolling current as though leaving the story of Gandhi, going far out, away from the great river, reaching higher and higher, through streaks of clouds as end titles begin.

And through them, once more we hear, dimly, reminiscently, through the rushing wind:

"At home *children* are writing 'essays' about him!" . . . the croaky voice singing, "God save our gracious King" . . . Dyer: "Sergeant Major—," the Sergeant Major: "Take aim!," Dyer: "Fire!," the sound of massed rifle fire, screams . . . "You are my best friend . . . my highest guru, and my sovereign lord." "Who the hell is he?," "I don't know, sir." "My name is Gandhi. Mohandas K. Gandhi." . . . the sound of rioting, women's screams, terror . . . "Find a child—a child whose mother and father have been killed. A little boy . . . about this high." . . . "He thinks he's failed." . . . "Long live Mahatma Gandhi! . . . Long live Mahatma Gandhi!"

The End

Selected Grove Press Paperbacks

B453   ARSAN, EMMANUELLE / Emmanuelle II / $3.50

E96   BECKETT, SAMUEL / Endgame / $2.95

B78   BECKETT, SAMUEL / Three Novels; Molloy, Malone Dies, The Unnamable / $4.95

E33   BECKETT, SAMUEL / Waiting for Godot / $2.95

B108   BRECHT, BERTOLT / Mother Courage and Her Children / $2.45

B115   BURROUGHS, WILLIAM S. / Naked Lunch / $2.95

E773   CLURMAN, HAROLD (Ed.) / Nine Plays of the Modern Theater (Waiting For Godot by Samuel Beckett, The Visit by Friedrich Dürrenmatt, Tango by Slawomir Mrozek, The Caucasian Chalk Circle by Bertolt Brecht, The Balcony by Jean Genet, Rhinoceros by Eugene Ionesco, American Buffalo by David Mamet, The Birthday Party by Harold Pinter, Rosencrantz and Guildenstern are Dead by Tom Stoppard) / $11.95

B342   FANON, FRANTZ / The Wretched of the Earth / $4.95

E792   GETTLEMAN, MARVIN, et. al., eds. / El Salvador: Central America in the New Cold War / $7.95

E697   MAMET, DAVID / American Buffalo / $3.95

E101   IONESCO, EUGENE / Four Plays (The Bald Soprano, The Lesson, The Chairs, and Jack, or The Submission) / $4.95

E259   IONESCO, EUGENE / Rhinoceros and Other Plays / $4.95

E697   MAMET, DAVID / American Buffalo / $ 3.95

B10   MILLER, HENRY / Tropic of Cancer / $3.95

B59   MILLER, HENRY / Tropic of Capricorn / $3.50

E411   PINTER, HAROLD / The Homecoming / $4.95

B438   REAGE, PAULINE / Story of O, Part II: Return to the Chateau / $2.95

E744   POMERANCE, BERNARD / The Elephant Man / $4.25

B313   SELBY, HUBERT / Last Exit to Brooklyn / $2.95

E763   SHAWN, WALLACE, and GREGORY, ANDRE / My Dinner with Andre / $5.95

E618   SNOW, EDGAR / Red Star Over China / $8.95

B319   STOPPARD, TOM / Rosencrantz and Guildenstern Are Dead / $2.95

B341   SUZUKI, D. T. / An Introduction to Zen Buddhism / $2.95

B474   TOOLE, JOHN KENNEDY / A Confederacy of Dunces / $3.95

GROVE PRESS, INC., 196 West Houston St., New York, N.Y. 10014